GENTLY DOWN
THE STREAM

GENTLY DOWN THE STREAM

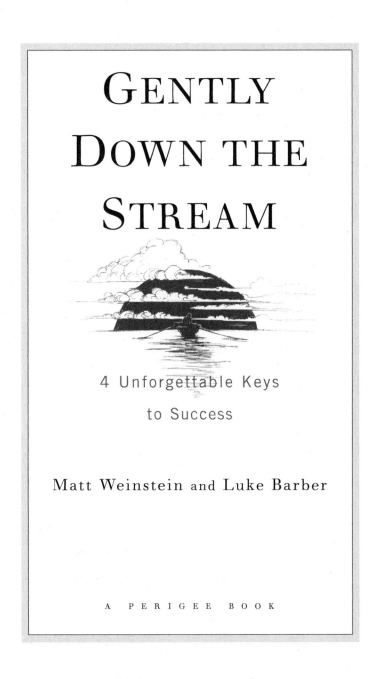

4 Unforgettable Keys
to Success

Matt Weinstein and Luke Barber

A   PERIGEE   BOOK

A PERIGEE BOOK
Published by the Penguin Group
Penguin Group (USA) Inc.
375 Hudson Street, New York, New York 10014, USA

Penguin Group (Canada), 90 Eglinton Avenue East, Suite 700, Toronto, Ontario M4P
2Y3, Canada (a division of Pearson Penguin Canada Inc.)
Penguin Books Ltd., 80 Strand, London WC2R 0RL, England
Penguin Group Ireland, 25 St. Stephen's Green, Dublin 2, Ireland (a division of Penguin
Books Ltd.)
Penguin Group (Australia), 250 Camberwell Road, Camberwell, Victoria 3124, Australia
(a division of Pearson Australia Group Pty. Ltd.)
Penguin Books India Pvt. Ltd., 11 Community Centre, Panchsheel Park, New Delhi—110
017, India
Penguin Group (NZ), Cnr. Airborne and Rosedale Roads, Albany, Auckland 1310, New
Zealand (a division of Pearson New Zealand Ltd.)
Penguin Books (South Africa) (Pty.) Ltd., 24 Sturdee Avenue, Rosebank, Johannesburg
2196, South Africa

Penguin Books Ltd., Registered Offices: 80 Strand, London WC2R 0RL, England

While the authors have made every effort to provide accurate telephone numbers and Internet addresses at the time of publication, neither the publisher nor the authors assume
any responsibility for errors, or for changes that occur after publication. Further, the publisher does not have any control over and does not assume any responsibility for author or
third-party websites or their content.

Copyright © 2006 by Matt Weinstein and Luke Barber
Text design by Richard Oriolo

First edition: September 2006

Library of Congress Cataloging-in-Publication Data

Weinstein, Matt.
   Gently down the stream : four unforgettable keys to success in life and work / Matt
Weinstein and Luke Barber.— 1st ed.
      p. cm.
   ISBN 0-399-53282-X
   1. Success—Psychological aspects.   I. Barber, Luke.   II. Title.

BF637.S8W356 2006
158—dc22

2006044562

PRINTED IN THE UNITED STATES OF AMERICA

10   9   8   7   6   5   4   3   2   1

This book is dedicated to

Geneen, Barbara, Lee, and Joann—

whole and beautiful women whose sustaining love

has helped us in countless ways to flow ever

so gently down the stream.

Life is really simple, but we insist on
making it complex.
—CONFUCIUS

CONTENTS

PART III

Merrily, Merrily, Merrily, Merrily

PART IV

Life Is But a Dream

ACKNOWLEDGMENTS

ONE IDEA THAT we support in this book is that none of us will be able to row our way to genuine success alone. The full recognition of our interdependence helps us to understand that "perfection in one oarsman means nothing." Simply put, we need others. Space does not permit me to acknowledge all those who have supported my efforts through the years. I owe so much to so many people. I must at the very least, however, mention the following people who helped, in their own special ways, make this book a reality.

Many colleagues at Richland College, especially Steve Mittelstet, Janet James, Joyce McKnight-Williams, and Scott Shepard made important contributions. My friends, Marje and Dick Takei, Lynn and Arye Alexander, John Trickle, and Gary Verett all had a part in this work.

Our agent Brian DeFiore is the best. Brian is always deeply involved in many positive ways in the creation of our projects. Without his reliable perspective we would sink. Kate Garrick, Brian's able assistant, is a gem. Without our editor, John Duff, this book would have never come about, as it was his idea. I love working with John and his creative staff.

Lee Paez continues to be my steady and constant source of love and support. She is always my first reader, and blends so beautifully the roles of cheerleader and unrestrained critic. My children, Alicia Paez, Kevin Paez, and Rachel Barber continue to inspire me on a daily basis. I relearned during the writing of this book just how much they mean to me. I cannot imagine having a better friend and writing partner than Matt Weinstein. We work together like hand and glove, foot and shoe, milk and cookies, Lucy and Desi. I'm never sure who is which! I'm sure our books would be much longer if we spent more time writing and less time laughing. Someday we will write us yet another book.—LB

First of all, I would like to fondly remember Rex, the talking dog, who was the narrator of this book in its first draft. We thought it was a great idea to make a bridge between this book and our previous book *Dogs Don't Bite When a Growl Will Do*, and Rex performed that task admirably. When we showed the manuscript to our agent Brian DeFiore, his reaction was quite simple: "Lose the dog!" When we prevailed on him to show the manuscript to our editor John Duff, his response was equally clear. "Lose the dog!" They were right and we were wrong. Rest in Peace, Rex. May you have a second life in a future book that is yet undreamed.

John Duff heard our lecture on "The Four Unforgettable Principles" and immediately said, "You should write your next book about the row, row, row your boat principles." What a great idea!

My friends and colleagues Rick Curwin, Carla Rieger, and Sarah Fisk generously allowed us to tell their wonderful stories in this book.

Hameed Ali and Jeanne Hay introduced me to the concept of basic trust. It is through their inspired and heartfelt teachings that I was able to discover my own sense of basic trust.

My wife Geneen Roth, who is a fabulous writer herself, was once again my full-time muse and part-time editor on this book. She is a constant inspiration to me on so many levels, and I'm glad she liked what she read!

Finally, writing this book with my coauthor Luke Barber has once again been one of the great joys of my life. What fun we continue to have together! Life is truly a dream in his presence.—MW

The Four Keys
to Success

THROUGH THE YEARS, the participants in our programs and seminars have been interested in some basic guidelines to orient them in their quest for success. They have shared with us their experience with the "Eight Choices," the "Seven Habits," or the "Six Secrets" that they have found in other books. These ideas have helped and even inspired them, but the students have observed that most of these "simplifying ideas" are much too complicated—they are just too difficult to remember. A short time after they have read these books they are asking themselves, "Now, what was that secret number five again?"

So, one day the two of us were talking about how to create a set of simple guides to help people on their journey to success. Luke, being a philosopher by nature and profession, suggested that if we were to develop such guidelines we should heed the words of the twentieth-century philosopher Ludwig Wittgenstein: "the aspects of things that are most important to us are hidden because of their simplicity and familiarity."

"Yes!" agreed Matt enthusiastically. "If we develop some guiding principles for success, they need to be easy to remember, but have an unexpected depth to them." As a teacher of improvisation and a great believer in the idea of seeing familiar things with fresh eyes, Matt offered another favored quote, this from the nineteenth-century philosopher Arthur Schopenhauer: "Thus the task is not so much to see what no one yet has seen, but to think what nobody yet has thought about that which everybody sees."

"Ah," muttered Luke appreciatively. "So then, if we can find something that everyone already thinks they know all about, but help them to look at it in a new way . . ."

In that moment, the four simple principles set forth in this book miraculously revealed themselves to us. As we tell people in our audiences, you won't have to write these down, you don't have to take any notes—we promise that these four principles are so simple, so fundamentally engaging (with an emphasis on the "fun"), and so recognizable, that two weeks from now you will have no difficulty remembering them. In fact, we guarantee that you will remember them for the rest of your life!

Here are the four remarkable and unforgettable keys to success:

1) Row, row, row your boat

2) Gently down the stream

3) Merrily, merrily, merrily, merrily

4) Life is but a dream

The usual reaction when people first hear these four principles is always the same: appreciative, but tentative, laughter. However, when they look in more detail and see what these lines have to teach them about achieving success, the laughter transforms into thoughtful reflection. After a few minutes of discussion, these same people begin to appreciate that we are, in fact, quite serious about the value of these keys to success.

These four lines provide a simple yet powerful and profound guide to successful living. These straightforward ideas can help you to reduce stress, create joy, enhance motivation, foster teamwork, ensure satisfaction in your work, and much, much more. In short, they are uncomplicated guides for finding success and happiness in life.

By focusing on these four lines as essential keys to success and happiness, this book will help you apply them to all aspects of your life, whether at work, in personal relationships, or in any other component of daily living. The two of us are convinced that the same skills for living that lead to success in one context apply equally in others. The same skills that make you successful at work will assist you in being better parents, partners, friends, and community members.

Most people are familiar with "Row, Row, Row Your Boat" as a "round"—a song that can be entered at any of its lines. That is, we believe, also one of the advantages of this book. All four of the song's lines are interconnected. So it doesn't matter if you enter this book with an interest in increasing the joy in your life and having more fun at work (*Merrily, Merrily, Merrily, Merrily*), reducing stress and living more peacefully (*Gently Down the Stream*), or embracing personal action and responsibility (*Row, Row, Row Your Boat*)—you'll find that each key flows easily into all of the others. Once you have mastered these three fundamental approaches to living, you will find that every aspect of your life can be like a dream come true!

This introduction is the only place where we use the "we" voice—the rest of the book is written in the first person. As is our convention in the other books we have written together, we make no distinction between Luke's experiences and Matt's experiences.

There is one big advantage to using the "we" voice in this introduction, however. There are three of us here right now—the two of us, and you—and three is the perfect number to start singing a fun round like "Row, Row, Row Your Boat." So . . . let's get started!

LUKE BARBER   MATT WEINSTEIN
Eugene, Oregon   *Berkeley, California*

PART I

ROW, ROW, ROW YOUR BOAT

People who are successful play an active role in the creation of their own reality. If you want to be successful in life, then you must be willing to take an ongoing and energetic role in making it happen.

ONE

Don't Just Sit There, Do Something!

Even if you are on the right track, you will get run over if you just sit there.

—WILL ROGERS

I ALWAYS LIKED THE story of the faithful man who prayed day after day for months on end that he might win the lottery. He prayed with passion, conviction, dedication, and hope. He was not the least bit deterred when months of prayer became years of prayer without any success. The man did not win the lottery—not even a small prize—not even once. Finally, in a state of great hopelessness, he turned to the skies and shouted, "God, I am a good and faithful man. I never harmed anyone. I worship and pray regularly. All I have ever asked of you is to let me win the lottery, just one time!" Suddenly, there was a loud clap of thunder and a booming voice replied from the heavens: "Hey! Meet me halfway here. Buy a ticket, already!"

The sixteenth-century writer Sir Thomas More gave voice to a much wiser and more realistic version of this same prayer: "The things, good Lord, which we pray for, give us the grace to labor for." The wisdom of this prayer is that it recognizes that success in life is not just handed to you—rather, you have to participate in your own success.

Success is not something that just happens to some people and doesn't happen to others. Each of us must be willing to take personal responsibility for the design and construction of our lives—at home, at work, and in all other aspects of our lives. If we are not successful, then we must be willing to hold ourselves accountable. Blaming others for our own lack of success has never achieved anything. In short, we must become active participants in the creation of our own success.

There are many different doorways to success. What should you do to be successful? For a start, just do what's right in front of you right now. If you're in a boat, for example, you need to row that boat. You don't just row it once, you need to row, row, and row it consistently. If, for example, you want your work environment to be a joyful place that nourishes both you and your coworkers, then you have to be active and energetic in making that happen. Few things can help us more in our lives than realizing that we don't just play a minor role in the story that is our lives. We have the lead role and what happens is monumentally influenced by the reality that we create.

A perfect example of this truth is illustrated in a story my friend Rick Curwin told me. Rick is a management consultant who travels virtually everywhere with his adorable lapdog, Otis. One day while taking a walk through Golden Gate Park in San Francisco, Rick spotted a woman relaxing against a large boulder. She was, he said, the most beautiful woman he had ever seen. As Rick looked around more carefully, he noticed a group of people huddled around a battery of lights set up to illuminate a nearby outcropping of rocks, and he realized that this woman must be a professional model on a break from a photo shoot.

"Normally a woman like that wouldn't even give me the time of day," Rick confided to me. "She had that kind of 'Don't bother me, I'm bored with you already, I'm too cool to exist' look in her eyes. She definitely knew that she was one of the 'Beautiful People.' I wanted to meet her, but I figured I would just walk on by. Then, I happened to think of my secret weapon—my dog, Otis! When Otis bats his long eyelashes at you, he is irresistible."

Sure enough, as Rick approached the woman with Otis in the lead, her eyes lit up at the sight of the little dog waddling toward her. She bent down to pet him. "What an adorable dog!" she exclaimed.

"If you can guess my dog's name I'll buy you dinner tonight," Rick said playfully.

"I'm not interested," replied the model.

"That's right! You got it! That's his name!" responded Rick enthusiastically.

There was a brief moment of suspicious silence between them, and then the model began laughing. "I'm still not interested!" she said emphatically through her laughter.

"Maybe I didn't get a date with this gorgeous woman," Rick told me later. "But I had fun, and she did, too. And in truth I probably had more fun in those few minutes than I would have had if she had actually agreed to go out on a date with me. Besides that, I saved the price of a fancy meal!"

Rick's story shows how easy it can be for us to create joy and laughter in our lives if we can remember not to just sit there but, instead, to do something. One of the things that I appreciate about this story is that it demonstrates that when we bring happiness to ourselves and others, we just keep on reaping the benefits. As Rick recounted his tale to me, I could tell that he was experiencing great joy in the retelling of the story. Once a playful interaction has passed, it can live on many more times in the retelling.

Some might argue that Rick was not successful with the woman at all; yet, as Rick told me the story, it certainly sounded like success to me. Rick's attitude was one of triumph rather than failure, and the attitude that we have about our experiences is a much better indication of our success than any other measure.

Every person's life has a unique formula for creating success. This book will help you answer important questions about how to construct your own variety of success, happiness, and joy in your life, and especially your life at work. In these pages you will discover your own answers to many questions.

How am I going to produce the kind of success that I am really after?

What am I going to do to generate more happiness in my life?

How can I craft a reality that will bring me peace and joy in my life every day?

What am I going to do to get actively involved in creating more success in my life and at work?

How can my life be a dream come true?

You're in the boat. It's time to row!

Don't Just Do Something, Sit There!

Vision without action is a daydream.
Action without vision is a nightmare.

—JAPANESE PROVERB

F OR MANY DECADES I have had a good laugh at the numerous "good news and bad news" jokes that have come my way. One in particular that has really stuck around in my family involves an airline pilot who startled the passengers with the following midflight announcement: "Ladies and gentlemen, this is your captain speaking. I hope you are having a pleasant flight. I have good news and bad news for you today. The bad news is that we are hopelessly lost. Neither the copilot nor I have the slightest clue where we are. The good news is that we are making excellent time!"

Whenever I am lost, on the wrong track, or in any way confused about the right direction to take in my life, I can count on my wife to provide me with the good news——"Yes, sweetheart, and you are making excellent time!" Her comment is always good for a much-needed laugh, and the realization that I am making great time to who-knows-where never fails to gives me pause.

Rowing your boat with vigor and consistency is an essential element in achieving success in life and at work. You can't just sit there, you have to do something. On the other hand, rowing with energy, vitality, and steadiness gets you absolutely nowhere if you are rowing on only one side of the boat. Even a novice in a rowboat quickly learns that without paying attention to both sides of the boat, you will end up going in circles. Furthermore, even if you row with great consistency and energy on both sides of the boat, you might as well be going in circles if you don't know where you are going.

It is fruitless to be making good time without knowing our destination. As the ancient proverb tells us, "a bird with one wing cannot fly." If we want to fly we need to have two wings beating in harmony: a wing of wise action and also a wing of wise direction.

The ancient Chinese sage Confucius suggested that the noblest way to learn wisdom is reflection. In other words, sometimes we need to stop all the doing and "just sit there." We need to get clear about where we want to go. We need to reflect on our goals and be clear about what success will actually look like for us. We need to clarify our destination and understand the route that will take us there.

Many of us live with only vague notions of what we want. We have fuzzy dreams of where we are going and hazy hopes for the future. When we aren't very clear about where we want to go, we often head for someone else's image of success. As one of my wisest teachers, my dear uncle Joe, used to say, "The most important thing about having goals is that they are your own." When we follow someone else's goals, we may end up making excellent time, but we are still lost.

People who are successful always have clear goals on which they stay focused. When people who are not clear about where they are going experience failure, it often becomes a stopping point for them. On the other hand, failure does not deter those who are committed to their own unique vision of success. As the old saying tells us, "the world steps aside for those who know where they are going."

There are a few questions that may be helpful as you think about what success might look like for you.

Have I taken some time to be still and really reflect upon where I want to be in my life?

Am I sure that my image of success is really mine?

If so, do I have a clear vision of how to get there?

Unless the answer to all three of these questions is an unqualified "Yes," then it may be a good time to pull in the oars and just sit there for a while!

THREE

A Very Big Box

Every man takes the limits of his own field
of vision for the limits of the world.
—ARTHUR SCHOPENHAUER

L ATELY I HAVE been told at every turn that I must learn to "think outside the box." Frankly, anytime I hear the phrase—whether from a corporate or educational leader, a leadership trainer, an organizational guru, or anyone else—my first suspicion is that I am listening to someone who is so deeply ensconced within his own small box that he cannot see the forest for the cardboard.

As human beings, we cannot escape having frames of reference, and it is not possible to think outside your own frame of reference. We all need to have a worldview, which means that we must all think from within our own "box." It's just not possible to "think outside the box." The important thing is to be deeply aware that most of us prefer the safety of small boxes, and we must constantly strive to expand our worldview.

When we learn to look at things in new and unexpected ways, we begin to expand our way of seeing the world beyond its usual limits and constraints. This is not always easy to do, however. When we think creatively and open ourselves fully to new possibilities, we need—to some degree—to be willing to give up our usual feelings of comfort and safety in what we know. We need to surf the edge of our experience.

A short time ago, a student said to me that he finally understood what I was trying to do. He said that at first he thought I was trying to teach him to "think outside the box," and he wasn't having much success figuring out how to do it. "Now I understand," he said, "that you just wanted me to expand my capacity for thinking." He paused for several thoughtful moments and then said, "It's just that I had no idea how very big the box could be!"

When we are rowing our boat in the direction of success, it is important to remember that the limited way we see the world can keep us from envisioning all the possibilities that are available to us.

For example, Carla Rieger, who is a trainer for my company, Playfair, Inc., was able to expand her perception of reality in a very dramatic fashion. Carla was on a business trip to Montana, where she had presented a very successful program for the entire new student class at Montana Technical University. She was flushed with energy from the success of the program, and since she had a few hours to herself Carla decided to go for a jog in a nearby park before checking out of her hotel.

She had an exhilarating run and was feeling great until she returned to her rental car and could not find the car key. Obviously it had fallen out somewhere during her run.

Carla realized she needed to contact the rental company, but her wallet and her cell phone were locked inside the car. There was a pay phone in the park, but unfortunately she had no money, and the park was virtually deserted. She looked along the row of benches to see if there was anyone from whom she could borrow the price of a phone call. That's when her heart sank. There were only two other people in the park. One was an old man feeding the pigeons, who looked like he could hardly spare any change. The other was a young man, his hair in a Mohawk, tattoos up and down his arms, menace radiating out in all directions from his sneering face.

After considering her choices, Carla did what most people would do and made a beeline for the old man. Surely of the two he was her best hope for help. She laid out her sorrowful tale and asked him for change for the phone. "Yes, I believe I do have a quarter, but it's my last one," he told her reluctantly. Carla looked at him expectantly, and after a moment's hesitation he reached inside his tattered old pants and produced a coin.

"As soon as I can get inside my car, I'll pay you back, I promise," she told him. "Thank you, thank you, you saved my life!"

Carla sprinted over to the pay phone and dialed the rental car company. The agent at the other end of the line did not have good news for her. "No, we don't have any spare keys," she said without sympathy. "We can send a locksmith over to you, but you'll have to pay for it."

"That's fine," countered Carla. "How fast can a locksmith get here?"

"Oh, in a couple or three hours, I guess. We're way busy over here right now."

"What?" shrieked Carla. "That won't work. My plane is leaving in two hours. I have to make that plane!"

"That's the best I can do for you right now."

"That's outrageous! Haven't you ever heard of customer service? I want to speak to your manager!"

"Gotta go now." With that the line went dead.

Carla hung up the phone in despair. Now she didn't even have money for another phone call. She looked over at the young man, her last hope for salvation. He looked about nineteen years old, and he was straddling the back of a bench, chain-smoking cigarettes and gazing off into the distance. She knew that asking him for money was out of the question. He wasn't the type of person who gave away money to strangers—he was the type of person who took money from strangers!

If she told him her story he'd probably laugh in her face. He was probably the worst possible person to ask for help in this kind of situation. At least that's the story, Carla realized, that most people would likely tell themselves. "What's another way," she wondered to herself, "that I can approach this tough guy, so that he might be helpful to me?" At that moment Carla was able to break free of her expected and predictable thinking. She was able to expand the way she viewed the world.

She walked over to the angry-looking young man, and he stared at her with evident hostility, clearly annoyed at having to deal with her. Carla's first few words changed all that. "I'll give you twenty bucks to break into my car!" she offered.

"Cool!" he replied.

He reached inside his jacket and pulled out just the right tool for the occasion, a thin plastic jimmy. Two minutes later he had effortlessly popped the lock on the rental car.

"That was great!" Carla said enthusiastically. Then she gave him thirty dollars instead of the promised twenty.

"I like it a lot better this way," he laughed as he walked back to the bench.

"Another satisfied customer," Carla called after him playfully.

He turned back to look at her one last time, and nodded solemnly. "Anytime."

Carla paid back the old man, and made her plane with time to spare.

What Carla discovered is that our expectations can often keep us stuck in place. Sometimes the solution we need is right before our eyes, but we can't see it because we are caught in a trance of only seeing things in one expected way. When Carla first looked at the young man, she thought "Danger here!" It did not occur to her to look at the same menacing figure and think, "My savior!" It was only when Carla was able to look at the situation in a new way that she was able to realize that the perfect solution to her problem was standing right in front of her, disguised as something else.

When we can open ourselves up to looking for solutions that are counterintuitive, incongruous, and even ridiculous, we will often discover a result that makes our lives better and more successful. This is not always a difficult process to achieve; rather, it is quite a natural one. Being keenly aware that you are probably trapped inside your own small box is the first step toward expanding your vision. Once you start thinking to yourself, "There has to be another way to look at this!" then you are halfway there. When you have the realization of the limitations of your worldview firmly in mind, you will discover a natural loosening of the bonds of your creative thinking. As you relax into the possibility that there are alternative solutions to your problems, a new world of fresh possibilities from which to choose can then emerge.

The key to success comes in a very large box.

FOUR

Think Like a Child

Grown men can learn from very little children for
the hearts of little children are pure. Therefore, the
Great Spirit may show to them many things which
older people miss.

—BLACK ELK

I AM ASSUMING THAT after reading the last chapter you are interested in the possibility of expanding your frame of reference, so that you can view the world from multiple perspectives. The big question, then, is how, exactly, do you do that? Where can you look for mentors to help you on your quest? Fortunately, you already have a great role model readily available—the nearest child!

I remember some years back driving down the highway with my young nephew—he couldn't have been more than four or five years old. He was leaning over the front seat with his fist beneath his chin, staring into space, deep in thought. After riding for a long time in silence, he said, "You know, if it weren't for gravity we would be flying now!" Young children have a creative way of seeing the world that is way beyond the kind of thinking that most of us do.

When you practice thinking more like a child, you will avoid the inclination to believe that reality is limited and small. You will become more open to alternatives. You will see beyond the norm. You will become a visionary!

Niels Bohr, the Danish physicist and Nobel Prize winner, exhibited exactly these qualities as a young student. Bohr had been asked on an examination to show how it was possible to determine the height of a building with the aid of a barometer. His answer was that one could take the barometer to the top of the building, attach a long rope to it, lower it to the street, and measure the length of the rope, which would be the same as the height of the building.

Bohr's professor took the position that the answer did not show competence in physics and he was threatening to give Bohr a zero for the answer; however, Bohr argued that he deserved a perfect score. He was then given another opportunity to answer the question, but this time he must demonstrate knowledge of physics. So the young Bohr wrote that one could take the barometer to the top of the building, drop it, and time its fall with a stopwatch. One could then use a mathematical formula to calculate the height of the building.

His professor ultimately gave up and awarded almost full credit for the answer. Bohr reportedly said that he had many other solutions, but that his favorite was that he could go to the superintendent of the building and offer him a fine new barometer if he would tell him the height of the building. Bohr said that he knew the "correct" answer that he was expected to give; however, he was fed up with teachers trying to teach him how to think. He felt that they weren't really teaching him how to think at all—they were trying to narrow his thinking into predictable and anticipated categories.

Bohr's story demonstrates the kind of thinking that we should all prize—being able to see things from multiple perspectives, being fully open to different approaches and answers, and living with awakened creativity. This kind of thinking is characteristic of a child. When we learn to think like a child, we will look at the world with deep wonder, fresh eyes, profound innocence, and appreciation for the immeasurable possibilities and opportunities of life. This is the kind of thinking that can help you to become more successful in all your endeavors. It is a quality that needs to be nourished and developed.

FIVE

Carmichael Did It

*You can't keep blaming yourself. Just blame
yourself once, and move on.*

—HOMER SIMPSON

FOR MANY YEARS we have had a lighthearted blame
game in my family. Whatever is involved—from leaving
the milk out of the refrigerator to passing gas in public—
we always identify the guilty culprit the same way: "Carmichael
did it!" Carmichael is the invisible leprechaun member of the
family who eats the last piece of cake, uses the last piece of toilet
paper without replacing the roll, or leaves the water sprinkler running all night. You can count on a dependable response to questions like, "Who moved my briefcase?" or "Who left these dirty
towels on the bathroom floor?" The guilty party always responds,
"Carmichael did it."

Our family game is in reality a fun way of accepting responsibility rather than passing it on. It is a way of sheepishly admitting, "I did it." Making excuses when things go wrong and blaming others for our choices are fairly common human traits. These traits are born out of the desire to let someone else do the rowing of the boat while we angle for a free ride.

I have a professor friend who noticed an incredibly high correlation between his assigning an examination and all sorts of student ills. All he had to do was assign an exam, and the day of the test would bring about numerous deaths of relatives, a bunch of auto accidents, and all sorts of mysterious plagues and diseases. He once said that the best excuse he ever heard was from a student who had missed the exam completely. At the beginning of the next class, the student reported that he had suffered a fatal accident on the way to the test!

All of us do at times have legitimate reasons why we fail at one thing or another. It is important to keep in mind, however, that the practice of looking for excuses for failure can become habitual—a habit we want to avoid. When we row our boat toward success, we want to leave excuses behind in our wake. The habit we want to form, instead, is the practice of taking personal responsibility.

Taking personal responsibility involves accepting accountability for our own choices and not getting caught up in the blame game. Taking personal responsibility means not fooling ourselves about ourselves. It means that we are deeply aware of our part in things. We don't fool ourselves about our role in failures, and we don't fool ourselves about our role in successes. We are quick to be proactive rather than helpless when it comes to making things happen. All these things are important components of living responsibly.

Among the most successful college presidents in the United States is Steve Mittelstet of Richland College in Dallas, where for many years I have been a member of the faculty. If you shadow President Mittelstet for a week, then you will, naturally, observe him doing many of the jobs that you would expect of a college CEO—conducting meetings, working with his administrative team to make high-pressure decisions, meeting with members of the community. However, you will also find him doing things like picking up a piece of litter and depositing it in a trash receptacle, walking with a new student to show her the way to the college bookstore, and taking down an outdated sign in the Student Center. That's because he doesn't ever ask, "Whose job is this?" He sees only that there are jobs to be done and he takes personal responsibility for getting them done.

This is not to be confused with micromanagement. He simply views himself as a member of a team. As he says, "If you are a member of the Richland team, then you know that we all have much meaningful work to do, from teaching students in the classrooms to weeding our gardens. As we work together on the team, each one of us is responsible for the success of the whole and the success of each part."

As you can imagine, when the leader of an organization does his or her job in this way, it cannot help but influence everyone within the organization. We do not have to be the CEO, however, to take personal responsibility or to have an effect upon everyone around us. Taking responsibility and being personally accountable are infectious behaviors. When we row, row, row our boat with passion and enthusiasm, we make those around us want to pick up an oar and join in.

SIX

It's Just That Simple

*The business schools reward difficult complex
behavior more than simple behavior, but simple
behavior is more effective.*

—WARREN BUFFETT

BEING AN ACTIVE participant in creating our own happiness and success at work is not necessarily a complex undertaking. Oftentimes it can be rather simple. I recently received a letter from Susan Clarke, a past participant in one of my stress reduction workshops. Susan, the manager of a large restaurant in Dallas, recounted a story that clearly demonstrates how simple rowing one's boat can be.

Susan was having a "day from hell" at work. Everything that could go wrong did go wrong. Her patrons were being served the wrong meals. Several employees had called in sick. Dishes were dropped and broken, and there had been a small kitchen fire. She found herself wondering, "What next?"

Then Susan remembered an exercise that we had done in the workshop. She gathered her entire staff in the kitchen and said, "This is only going to take a minute, but I need everyone's undivided attention for the next sixty seconds!" By the expressions on her workers' faces, she could tell that they were worried that she was about to "read them the riot act." Several looked nervously at their feet as they prepared for a royal chewing out.

Susan began her talk in a calm voice. "We all know that this has been a horrible day for us so far. Well, I've learned that sometimes you just have to shake it off and get on with your life, so that's what I am going to do!" At this point Susan began to quiver and shake like a dog coming in out of the rain, as if she were shaking off all the pesky annoyances and problems of the day.

She continued to squirm around madly for about fifteen seconds. By this point the earlier looks of apprehension had transformed into looks of amazement. "At first they were looking at me like I had totally lost it," she said, "but when they saw the smile on my face, they all began to laugh and clap their hands."

Susan finished off her own version of how to be a motivational manager with some marching orders. "Okay, that should do it. Let's all just shake it off and get back to work."

Susan wrote that her brief shaking fit transformed the entire restaurant. In a very short time she noticed that almost everyone on her staff was smiling and feeling upbeat. Before long she could see that this attitude was being transmitted to the patrons. What had been one of the worst workdays of her life had suddenly become one of the best. She concluded her letter with the phrase: "It was just that simple!"

Many of us are unable to shake off the little problems in our everyday life at work. What we may not realize is that carrying these petty tribulations around with us has a way of keeping us stuck in pessimism and negativity. Instead of being active in creating happiness and joy at work, we soon find ourselves rowing furiously upstream.

Susan's experience can teach us a couple of simple but important things about working with difficult situations. First, we do have a choice to do something about the situation when things are not going so well. We always have the ability to transform situations in our lives in powerful but simple ways. Rowing one's own boat is an activity that does not allow us to just sit there. It requires energy, so we are going to have to do something different if we want things to change.

The second thing that we can learn from Susan's experience is about the relationship of mind, body, and spirit. Our inner states can influence our physical states, and the reverse is also true. Susan made her experience physical. Had she simply said to her employees, "Okay, guys, we have had a really bad day. Let's shake it off and do better," my suspicion is that not much would have changed. The fact that she expressed the idea in a fun and physical manner made all the difference.

The way Susan handled the negative experience her employees were having that day brought out laughter and lightness. Her physical manifestation of shaking off her problems gave some much-needed mental relief to everyone involved. In rowing her boat in a new direction, she was able to get others rowing along as well. Susan was right. Sometimes it is just that simple.

SEVEN

You Are Not Alone

Coming together is a beginning, staying together is progress, and working together is success.

—Henry Ford

I N   N O   O T H E R sport is the word *team* so meaningful as in crew. Together in a shell, eight oars and eight sliding seats act as bindings—stroke to seven, seven to six, six to five . . . all the way to the bow. One rower's demon haunts the entire boat; perfection in one oarsman means nothing. A set boat and solid row is achieved solely when eight minds think identically, eight bodies melt together to form one machine." These words, from an essay entitled "Why I Love My Coxswain" by Erin Walker, capture an important facet of how we row our way to success—you are not alone in the boat.

Often after I talk with audiences about the need to "row, row, row your boat," I am approached by people who tell me that they "totally agree" with my metaphor. They go on to tell me how keenly aware they are that in the world—especially the business world—success is about ruthless competition. They see the world as a zero-sum game with winners dominating losers. The world for them is all about a "dog eat dog" and "survival of the fittest" reality. Not only have they misunderstood my presentation, I believe that their metaphors from nature are wrong, as well.

I was fortunate in the past to be a presenter numerous times with the famed British-American professor and anthropologist Ashley Montagu. I always loved his gentle warmth and great humor. I also appreciated his scholarly evidence that the natural world is much more cooperative than ruthless. Professor Montagu often talked about our strong drives toward social and cooperative behavior. He argued that in our biological and social evolution, human beings owe much more of our success as a species to our drive to cooperate than to any other natural force.

I am not opposed to all competition. I have been for a long time a competitive athlete myself. On the other hand, I am convinced that, rather than ruthless competition, it is our capacity to cooperate that will ensure authentic success. In a profound way we are connected to other people. In virtually every aspect of our lives we are interdependent. We need other people, and they need us.

Sometimes, however, we must work in situations that make us feel isolated. Even in those situations we can realize that solitude does not necessarily mean that we are truly alone. We may have to make a special effort to see the connections and to stay connected with our support network—but it is always worth the effort.

To cite one example, my company, Playfair, is a team-building organization whose employees, ironically enough, work mostly solo. As these Playfair trainers crisscross North America, they have developed a variety of strategies for staying in touch and supporting each other.

Sarah Fisk, one of the Playfair trainers, was in the middle of an extended road trip and, in her own words, "completely over-whelmed and freaked out by the number of things on my plate." That night, Sarah felt too wound up to sleep when she checked in to her room in a small-town motel.

While surfing the television, she discovered there was a channel on cable TV she had never seen before devoted entirely to fishing. This struck her as funny, so while checking in with the Playfair internal voice-mail network she left a message for fellow Playfair facilitator Nate Sears. "I was commiserating with Nate on the voice-mail about being road weary, and I mentioned this discovery of the Fishing Channel as a sort of a silver lining to being stuck in a podunk motel in the middle of rural No-idea-where-I-am-ville.

"A few minutes later he called back and left me a message that said he was also up in the middle of the night, also in the middle of nowhere, watching the Macramé Channel. I laughed myself to sleep that night, and we still laugh about it."

With the help of her distant teammate, Sarah realized that she was part of a team that reached out to support its far-flung members as they moved their organization toward success. Even in her isolation she could feel that she was not alone.

None of us will be able to row our way to genuine success without the help of other people. There is no point in trying to row it alone. The full recognition of our interdependence helps us to understand that "perfection in one oarsman means nothing."

EIGHT

Seeing Is Believing

Forever is composed of nows.

—EMILY DICKINSON

WE HAVE ALL heard the notion that "seeing is believing," and that "the proof of the pudding is in the eating." I will be the first to acknowledge that ultimately, results are of enormous importance. Yes, I have also heard the cliché that "life is a journey and not the destination." However, if we need to row from one side of the lake to the other, then it is important that we actually arrive on the other side. We may row actively, joyfully, and with full personal responsibility for the outcome, but if we don't make it to the opposite shore, then something is not quite right.

For example, I have a goal of finishing this chapter and, ultimately, the whole book. It simply wouldn't do if I don't ever finish the chapter. What would my editor say if the chapter just suddenly stopped midsentence? Perhaps I'll give it a try and find out. If my editor complains, I can always respond, "It's the journey and not the destination!"

Although it is true that achieving our desired result is an essential part of measuring our success in life, we don't want to judge something as complex as success simply on our ability to reach the other shore. It is important to remember that there are also many little successes available to us in each moment along the way. In short, success in life is both the journey and the destination.

A major part of my life has been my avocation as a runner. Of course, my running was part of an effort to maintain a decent level of fitness; however, the way that I approached running was much more than simply jogging a bit to stay in shape. I ran with passion and competitive zeal.

Very soon after I began running seriously, I started to run marathons. My first few marathons were fine, but after the first success I was not much satisfied with simply finishing the race. I wanted to continually improve my time. I did improve my times in the next three attempts, but then I hit a plateau. I had set myself a goal of running a sub-three-hour marathon, and I started holding as a failure anything less than that.

After numerous "failures," I was getting very discouraged. I was scheduled, however, to run in the Dallas White Rock Marathon, and my training had been going well, so I was very encouraged about my possibilities for success. "This will be the one," I thought.

The morning of the race was a very calm, crisp, cool December day in Dallas, perfect marathon weather. Early on I ran with confidence, but it was not to be my day. I hobbled the last couple of miles and crossed the finish line in three hours and eight minutes. I remember that I was disappointed with what was becoming a habit that I didn't enjoy at all—failure. I walked over to a park bench to rest and sat down next to another runner, who had clearly finished just seconds ahead of me.

He had a towel over his head and sweat was still pouring from his brow. He looked to be in a bit of pain, but he was obviously as happy as I was disappointed. I looked at him and, in an attempt to make conversation, asked, "So, do you know who won the race?"

He looked back at me and smiled and said, "I did!" It was clear to me that at least eighty runners had crossed the finish line before we did; however, he was able to see his run as a huge success where I could see mine as only failure.

I learned something important that day. It is essential to our success to have clear goals for the future. However, if we focus too much on our ultimate goal, then we may miss the little successes that we can experience every day.

I have had lots of freshman students tell me that their goal is to get a Ph.D., a goal which, of course, I want to acknowledge, honor, and respect. On the other hand, I want them to realize that there are many successes on papers, projects, courses, and in so many other things they can celebrate before they get that Ph.D.

So as we row our way to success it is important to keep an eye on the other shore; yet, we also want to realize the success that can be found in each well-made stroke.

NINE

Believing Is Seeing

*Sometimes I've believed as many as six impossible
things before breakfast.*

—THE WHITE QUEEN IN LEWIS CARROLL'S
THROUGH THE LOOKING GLASS

W HILE MOST PEOPLE will readily accept the
claim that "seeing is believing," they may underesti-
mate how often the opposite is also true: "believing is
seeing." Our beliefs can be a powerful force in shaping our reality.

I'm not a dedicated bird-watcher, but I do enjoy going out and
hiking in nature. If a bird shows up, then I'll watch it for a while.
I was once out bird-watching, however, with a friend who was an
enthusiastic and experienced birder. At one point during our day
together, I heard one particular bird flit through a tree nearby. My
birder friend, however, described with great detail this rare bird
he had just seen. He told me all about every facet of the bird

including the tiny markings on the chest and wings. He even provided a sampling of the unique call of the bird, which he was virtually certain he had just heard.

As I had noticed nothing but a bit of tree flitting, I was truly amazed at my companion's recitation. "How did you manage to gather all that remarkable information?" I asked. He looked back at me and said with all seriousness, "If I hadn't believed it, I probably wouldn't have seen it!"

I think there is a wonderful lesson here for those of us who are interested in success. Our beliefs about things greatly influence the way we experience reality. If we wake up on Monday morning and tell ourselves, "Oh, my God! This is going to be an awful week!" then we greatly enhance the possibility of living just that sort of week. If we say before a meeting, "I can't believe I have to spend two hours this morning with *those* people!" then we are already beginning to shape the reality we will experience in the meeting. Our mental attitude about our possibilities for success of any kind can play a powerful role in shaping the outcome.

Of course, we want to be somewhat realistic about our potential for success in any particular endeavor; however, in some ways being blissfully unaware of our limitations can have great value. When we believe that we can do virtually anything, we enhance the possibilities of that being so.

Many years ago I spent the day with Thomas Tutko, the man who is considered to be the inventor of sports psychology. He was a delightful, jovial man with sparkling Kris Kringle eyes. Tutko was working with numerous athletes and professional teams and had just published his classic work, *Sports Psyching*. He talked about the way in which the mental and the physical are intertwined and how each cell of our body is affected by what we envision.

At the time, I was training to run my tenth marathon and—as you learned in the previous chapter—had a longtime goal of breaking three hours. I kept coming close, but 3:05 was the best I had managed. One idea that Thomas Tutko stressed was that really successful athletes set extraordinarily high goals for themselves. A second idea was the psychological practice of mentally rehearsing the outcome that we want to achieve.

With this in mind I decided to forget about breaking three hours and decided instead to focus on running 2:50! I may be the worst artist who has ever graced the face of the earth, but I drew a picture of myself crossing under the clock at the finish line. The clock read 2:50:42. I posted the picture in my office and envisioned that finish line every day for weeks as I trained for the race. Two months later I passed under the finish line at the Woodlands Marathon, and as I glanced up the clock read 2:51:19.

This experience reinforced for me the enormous value of mentally rehearsing the successes that we want in life. We can't simply wait for the success to arrive in order to see it. We have to believe it first, as a way of helping us to see it. When we are rowing our way to success we must have a bold plan. Having a plan, however, is not enough. As we row, we must also believe.

TEN

The Barriers Come Down

Whatever affects one directly, affects all indirectly.
I can never be what I ought to be until you are
what you ought to be.

—MARTIN LUTHER KING, JR.

I ONCE ASKED THE CEO of a very successful company if there was any single thing to which she could attribute her success in business. After a moment of careful thought, she replied that a unique thing about her management style is that her organization is characterized by "chalk lines rather than fences." When I asked her to explain, she told me that good fences may make good neighbors, but barriers at work—between managers, coworkers, work groups, departments, customers—don't make for a healthy business climate.

She went on to explain that there is a need for some boundaries in the organization, but that in the healthiest corporate cultures those boundaries are easily crossed—like chalk lines. Fences, on the other hand, are difficult to cross and create an unnecessary separation between individuals and groups. We will be happier and more successful at work when we don't feel alienated from our coworkers.

This CEO isn't satisfied to simply let the work environment emerge without her active participation. She makes sure that she is hands-on in rowing the boat of her company.

There are all sorts of ways—big and small—that we can get actively involved in creating happiness and success at work for ourselves and our coworkers. National Trade Productions in Alexandria, Virginia, for example, created a permanent five-person "Smile Committee," whose mission is to lighten up the workplace. NTP president Tamara Christian funded the committee with a two-thousand-dollar yearly budget and told them to "go forth and have fun!"

The Smile Committee celebrates every known holiday and then invents some others for good measure. One of its most original contributions is a way of welcoming new employees into the company.

The Smile Committee members realized that new employees are bound to feel alienated on their first day at work, since they are not privy to the customs, secrets, and norms of the organization. So on a new employee's first day at NTP, the Smile team asks everyone in the organization to stop by and introduce themselves at the new person's desk.

The veteran employees are asked to bring along a card with their name and a little-known fact about themselves written on it. In that way the new employee immediately gets some "informational currency" about the coworkers and accelerates the process of feeling in the loop. By giving the veteran employees a creative way to disclose some personal information, this event starts off a welcoming relationship between new coworkers in an easy and effortless way.

The Smile Committee knows that it is important to reward employee participation in these little celebrations. So at the end of the day, the committee holds a drawing from the cards left on the new person's desk, and the lucky staffer who is selected wins a prize.

The Global Service Center (call center) of MasterCard International in St. Louis also found an excellent way to blur the traditional boundaries between management and staff when all the employees celebrated "Dress Your Supervisor Day." On this day all the managers with direct reports agreed to be dressed up by their employees. There were a few simple ground rules—no cross-gender dressing was allowed, and not too much skin could be showing.

When the big day arrived there were supervisors in pajamas, dressed as nuns, as biker chicks—and Elvis was definitely in the building. One group dressed up their manager as a mime, so they wouldn't have to listen to him talk! But apparently he really appreciated the idea—or at least that's what his employees imagined he was trying to communicate, as he walked around the office waving his arms, gesturing wildly, and making faces at everyone he met.

There is an artificial barrier that separates management from staff in any organization, and by participating in this event, the managers helped level the playing field. By their actions, they said, "Look, we're all human beings here. We spend more time with each other than with our flesh-and-blood families. We spend more time working together than we spend in all our other waking activities combined. If we can't have fun together and create a vibrant, human relationship at work, then we're going to wind up wasting most of our waking lives!"

In short, they said, "Bring down those barriers!"

PART II

GENTLY DOWN
THE STREAM

*People who are successful do not live with
tension and struggle. If you want to be
successful in life, there must be a flow to
your life. If you just relax into it,
the path to success will be revealed.*

ELEVEN

Chill!

It is better to have loafed and lost than to have never loafed at all.

—JAMES THURBER

I ONCE WENT TO visit a client, and when I looked in his office, he wasn't there. I went over to his assistant's desk and told her I was a bit early for my appointment. She laughed and said, "Oh, don't worry, he'll be back soon. He's just hanging out in the refrigerator."

"He's in the refrigerator?" I replied incredulously.

"Come on, I'll show you." I followed her down the hallway until we came to what turned out to be the company's "Stress-Free Zone." The room had a huge inflatable palm tree in one corner, and in the other corner was a "stress-reduction dummy," a large, inflatable punching bag with a sand-filled bottom. There were beanbag chairs on the floor for lounging about. I spotted my client relaxing in a hammock. As soon as he saw me, he leaped from the hammock and came over to shake my hand.

"Well, this looks like fun!" I exclaimed delightedly. Then I turned to his assistant. "But why did you say he was in the refrigerator?"

"Because that's what this place is called."

"And you call this the refrigerator because . . ."

"This is where we all go to chill!"

Going gently down the stream is a practice that can be learned. In many ways it is the practice of learning to chill out.

Most people have become so accustomed to living lives of struggle and tension that it may feel abnormal to follow any other path. It may seem very odd to relax in a hammock for a while at work or, for that matter, anywhere else. We have so much habitual energy around a Go! Go! Go! multitasking lifestyle that one of the most difficult things for us to do is to relax. However, learning to calm down, loosen up, let go, and flow more gently through our lives is one of the surest paths to authentic success.

One of my favorite Woody Allen quotes is that "death is nature's way of telling us to slow down." Unfortunately, it is true that too many people don't get the message to slow down and chill out until it is too late.

How refreshing it would be to work in a place that has a "refrigerator." How wonderful it would be to have wise employers who provide their employees with places to go to reduce stress and relax. Most likely, however, most of us will have to find other ways to make sure that we are flowing gently down the stream.

The world is a place that, in so many different ways—at work, at home, in our automobiles, and just about anywhere else we might show up—is much more like a frying pan than a refrigerator. If we are going to pull our lives out of the frying pan and into the fridge, then we are going to have to accept the difficult nature of the world. Instead of trying to fix the world, we can instead work on fixing ourselves in such a way that the world does not rob us of our calm and peace.

The chapters in this part of the book are intended to show how we can, regardless of the situation, jump out of the frying pan and into the refrigerator. On every day, in every way, and in every place, we can learn how to chill.

TWELVE

Walk This Way

All truly great thoughts are conceived by walking.

—FRIEDRICH NIETZSCHE

W HEN SOMEONE TELLS you, "Take a hike!" he usually means that he doesn't want you hanging around with him anymore. People are most likely to say something like this when they are angry or annoyed with you, and nobody likes to be on the receiving end of this kind of verbal abuse. These words are almost always spoken in an irritated tone of voice, but in fact this other person may be actually (although unintentionally) giving you some good advice. If he is angry with you, then chances are you are probably going to be angry with him quite soon, too. Especially when tempers are short, a simple thing like taking a walk can have wondrous results for your mental health.

My uncle Joe was the first one to teach me about the value of taking a walk. One day when I was about ten years old, my mother scolded me severely about some misbehavior on my part. I felt wronged, hurt, and angry. I went to my uncle Joe and told him exactly how I felt, which included some pretty nasty feelings toward my mom. After hearing just a bit of my woeful tale, he said simply, "I think we better take a walk." For many years to come, I noticed that taking a walk was my uncle's solution to virtually anything that troubled me or him.

Uncle Joe was middle-aged by the time I was born, and I saw him as the wise old philosopher in the family. I always went to him when I needed support or advice. He was a bachelor and lived in the front bedroom of my grandmother's house. At the age of seventy-five, he got married for the first time, because, he said, "There are a few things in life that ought to be tried at least once!" His change in marital status didn't change the fact that he walked every day of his life, right up until his accidental death, in his car, at age eighty-six.

On those walks with my uncle we rarely talked about much. He believed that problems were often solved in silence. One of his many favorite sayings was, "You're more likely to find heaven by walking than by talking."

Many years later, when I traveled to France to become a student of the Zen master Thich Nhat Hanh, I was reminded of my old uncle Joe's appreciation of walking. Thich Nhat Hanh often says that if you practice walking mindfully for a short time, then your life can be transformed. His practice is to walk very slowly, carefully putting one foot in front of the other, paying attention to every movement, to each breath, as your mind starts to relax.

Walking with our minds and our bodies in harmony can bring us peace and happiness and can help us to calm down and reevaluate the situation when we are upset. Walking with full awareness of our emotional state can also help us to transform our painful emotions into more nourishing ones. This is clearly a practice that can help us to go more gently down the stream.

Walking as a way of bringing more joy, peace, and calm into our lives is never about walking in order to get exercise or about getting to a specific destination. Intentional and attentive walking is much more about giving ourselves an emotional makeover. This alteration of our emotions is not, however, about simply forgetting or ignoring our feelings. It is about taking those negative feelings and transforming them. I notice that when I take the time to walk slowly, the whole world comes into focus in a different way. I can easily appreciate the things around me and my relationship to them. It feels good to be alive.

One of the things that I like most about walking our way to peace and calm is that it doesn't require that we go to a therapist's office, or to the woods, or to a mountaintop. Wherever we are we can take a walk. While we are waiting for our friends to meet us at the movies we can take a little, slow walk around the street corner. We can even walk in the hallway at work. For that matter, we can walk within our own cubicle, but we may need to take very tiny steps. Wherever we are we can know that peace and calm are just steps away.

The other thing I value about walking in peace is something that I also learned from my uncle Joe. You don't have to wait for something negative to happen to enjoy the happiness and peace that comes from thoughtful walking. Sometimes when we walked along in silence, my uncle would stop for a moment and smile. Then he would say, "I wonder what the poor people are doing now?" This was Uncle Joe's way of reminding me that—regardless of the material possessions that we did or did not have—we were rich in spirit as long as we could take a walk.

THIRTEEN

There Are Many Ways to Look at the Same Situation

No two men see the world exactly alike.

—Johann Wolfgang von Goethe

M Y POODLE CELESTE has had food allergies since she was a small puppy. When I took her to the vet the first time to talk about her problem, the vet said a very strange and amazing thing to me.

After giving the dog a very thorough examination she turned to me and said, "If you don't want this dog to have food allergies, the first thing you're going to have to do is change her name! What do you expect from a dog named Celeste—that name is so ethereal, so celestial. She needs a name that will bring her some grounding, bring her back to earth."

When I realized the vet was not kidding, I replied, "Forget it, I'm not changing her name. What else can I do for her?"

The vet recommended a new brand of hypoallergenic dog food, and later that day I was standing in line at the pet store holding a twenty-pound bag of the new food. The two customers in front of me were having an animated conversation, and I couldn't help eavesdropping. They were apparently husband and wife, and they were obviously schoolteachers. "Angel was acting out again, and I had to keep him after class," said the wife. "That's why I was so late."

I was only half-listening to their conversation, but the husband's reply completely caught my attention. "Yeah, that doesn't surprise me," he laughed. "Every time I've had a student named Angel, male or female, that student has been a terror. As soon as I see that I have a student named Angel in my class, I figure 'here comes trouble!'"

"Well, now," I thought to myself, "this is an interesting coincidence!" These two schoolteachers believe the exact opposite of what my vet believes about the power of names. They believe that their student Angel will behave in the opposite way to what his name suggests. My vet believes that my dog Celeste's name will bring about characteristics that are exactly the same as her name. These ideas can't both be true, can they? What about my own idea that names have nothing whatsoever to do with a person's behavior or a dog's health issues? Can all three of these opposing ideas be true at the same time?

Yes, in a certain sense they can because all three are clearly held as perceptions of reality. If you want to succeed in life and work, it is important to realize that reality is constantly fluid and changing, and that there is no one "true" way to see the world. Once we learn to be open and flexible to what is happening around us, once we learn to "go with the flow" of reality, then it is much easier for us to travel "gently down the stream." By letting go of our attachments that things need to be a certain way, we are less likely to be stressed out when things don't go the way we have planned, or when other people don't share our same version of reality. More important, perhaps, is that when we can learn to improvise in the moment, when we can learn to "see" things from more than one point of view, then solutions we never would have thought of to our problems are revealed to us.

Zen master Thich Nhat Hanh suggests that we should always be open to questioning our own notions about reality. He offers the idea that we place a sign both at home and at work to act as a simple reminder that things might not always be as we perceive them—a sign that says, ARE YOU SURE?

When we can approach life with openness and flexibility and don't need to be so sure about everything that we hold to be true, then we are much more likely to ease up on other people. When we ease up on others, we also have a tendency to ease up on ourselves. What results from easing up on ourselves is a feeling of inner calmness and a state of natural relaxedness. These are the very qualities of "lightening up" on oneself that are essential stepping-stones to achieving a successful and happy life.

FOURTEEN

We Get What
We Expect

*"Blessed is the man who expects nothing, for he shall
never be disappointed" was the ninth beatitude.*

—ALEXANDER POPE

I BROKE INTO A huge grin when I opened the envelope that told me I had been selected to receive a prestigious award from my professional association. The letter told me that I had to appear in person at a ceremony to accept the award, and in the months that followed, I came up with all sorts of fun ideas for my acceptance speech. On the evening of the ceremony, the audience was filled with hundreds of people from my profession, many of whom were friends of mine.

I had been sworn to secrecy not to reveal that I was one of the award recipients, so when my name was announced I got shocked looks from all the friends who were seated at my table. Naturally, all sorts of people came over to congratulate me afterward, and I was feeling quite elated about the whole thing.

When my friend Lee walked over to greet me after the ceremony, he said something that caught me completely off guard. "I couldn't believe it when they called your name!" he confided. "My jaw dropped open. I mean, can you believe they would actually give this award to you?"

"I know, can you believe it?" I agreed, trying my best to make a joke of what he had said. "These people must be out of their minds!" We had a good laugh together, and then he went off to say hello to some other friends. I thought no more about it that evening, but the next morning I woke up completely agitated. "Why did he say that to me?" I fumed. "What does he mean he can't believe they gave me that award? Doesn't he think I deserve it? What a lousy thing to say!"

It was still on my mind when I had lunch with a friend later that day, and I mentioned Lee's comments to her. "I'm not surprised to hear that, not at all," she counseled me. "Some people just can't handle seeing their friends get recognition, and it sounds like he is one of those people. They say that when you're in trouble, you find out who your real friends are . . . but it looks to me that when you're doing well, that's when you really find out! At least he was honest about it. You know, jealousy is a sad fact of life. You just have to live with it."

"Yeah," I thought bitterly, "what kind of friend is this guy, anyway? A real friend wouldn't try to ruin my moment in the sun."

Every time I saw Lee over the next few months I felt uncomfortable around him. I also felt a little embarrassed that he didn't think I was good enough to deserve the award. I found myself moving away from him at social occasions and finding excuses to walk away quickly whenever he approached me. It was more and more difficult for me to be in his presence, and so finally one day I decided to approach the subject head-on.

"Hey, do you remember that night I received the award?"

"Of course! What about it?"

"Do you remember what you said to me that night?"

"Remind me."

"You said that you couldn't believe that they would give me the award."

"Oh, yeah," he laughed. "I remember. That was incredible they gave it to you, wasn't it?"

"Well...," I said dubiously, "I don't know. Why do you think it was so incredible? What exactly did you mean by that?"

"What did I mean by that? I meant that up until that moment, I had assumed a handful of people running the organization gave the award to their close friends, or to the people who brownnosed them, or to the people that volunteered a lot of time to the association. I figured it didn't have anything to do with talent or with achievement but with how much you could suck up to the people in power. Then you got the award, and you didn't do any of that stuff, so I thought, well, maybe I'm wrong, maybe they actually gave the thing out on merit this time. Maybe they actually gave it to somebody who deserved it for once! Incredible!"

"Ahhh... so you meant that as a compliment?"

"Of course it's a compliment! What else could it be?"

"Oh, I mean, yes, of course it's a compliment, I mean, thanks a lot for saying that."

"You're welcome! Like I said, for once they got it right, buddy!"

I was amazed to realize how easily I had turned my friend's compliment into an insult. When there was a choice between interpreting Lee's remarks in a positive or a negative way, I didn't even notice the positive possibility—I went right for the negative! I had caused myself months of mental anguish.

Obviously I had found it difficult to take in so much positive feedback from my friends, and so I had undermined the situation for myself. At some level of consciousness I had expected that something would go wrong for me that night—and so I made sure that it did! Expectations play a powerful role in shaping our lives. Most of the time, we get whatever we expect. When we expect things to go wrong, whatever we hear sounds like bad news to us. We can make anything seem good or bad. It's all a matter of interpretation.

If we are going to travel gently down the stream, we need to manage our expectations instead of letting them manage us. An important first step is to remember, as we saw in the previous chapter, that there is no such thing as the "reality" of a given situation. Most everything can be interpreted in a number of different ways. Why not choose to have a positive expectation of things?

I have a friend who told me that he makes himself miserable every day because the first thought that comes into his head when he wakes up in the morning is "What's wrong, and who's to blame?" How much easier our lives would be if we could teach ourselves to wake up with the expectation that "Something's going to go right for me today!"

FIFTEEN

Developing Basic Trust

Our distrust is very expensive.

—Ralph Waldo Emerson

W HEN WE ALLOW our life to go gently down the stream, we trust that whatever happens to us is exactly what is supposed to happen. That doesn't mean that everything that happens will be "good" all the time. It simply means that we are open to the notion that we can find meaning and value in life no matter what happens to us at any given moment. It means that we are not invested in a particular outcome to any given situation. This kind of openness that our life is unfolding just the way it needs to for us to become ourselves is called "basic trust."

In the previous chapter, for example, I discovered that my

friend Lee was actually trying to give me a compliment and that gave the story a happy ending for me. What if I had instead discovered that my friend had meant just the opposite? What if, for whatever reason, he just didn't like seeing me get all that praise without trying to bring me back down to earth?

If I am constantly judging things as "good" or "bad" in a given situation, then I am lacking in basic trust. Basic trust isn't about good or bad. Going gently down the stream means I learn to flow without stress or tension no matter what my friend or anyone else has to say about my getting an award.

Having basic trust does not mean you have to pretend that everything is wonderful all the time. You just need to believe that whatever happens to you is exactly what is supposed to happen. You trust that whatever is happening to you right now, even if it is painful, is exactly right—that life is teaching you what you need to learn in this very moment.

Times of change and upheaval are the most difficult times to remember to relax into the flow of your life. When we can't see around the bend in the river, when we can't see where life is taking us or what is coming next, we feel uneasy. We begin rowing madly upstream, trying to return to familiar territory, splashing everyone around us, and drowning in stress and tension.

Yet once we understand that personal growth only happens when we expand our limits and move outside our comfort zone, then we can learn to welcome times of change and uncertainty. We can see those times as an opportunity for learning and growth. We can know that whatever happens will be useful to us in the long run. We can learn to be comfortable with discomfort.

There is a Zen story about a villager who was constantly complaining about everyone and everything. He was driving all his neighbors crazy. So the neighbors dragged him to the local monastery, where he had an audience with one of the monks.

"Are you really willing to change?" the monk asked him. "You can't change just because your neighbors don't like who you are. You have to change because you want to do something different with your life."

"I want to change," replied the man sorrowfully. "I know that I'm making myself miserable and making everyone around me miserable, too. That's just the way I am. That's the way I see the world."

"Ah," said the monk. "If you truly want to change, it can be done, but you must practice diligently. You must agree to this practice for the next six months. Whatever happens in your life you must greet with just two thoughts: 'Yes' and 'Thanks.' Regardless of how good or bad you think something that happens to you is, just respond with 'Yes, thanks!' If someone steals your chickens, you say, 'Yes, thanks!' If it rains all week when you want sunshine, you say, 'Yes, thanks!' No matter what happens, your only reaction is, 'Yes, thanks!' You do that for six months, then come back and see me."

For the next six months the villager dutifully carried out the monk's instructions. After a long day of work, it was 'Yes, thanks!' When mice ate his bread it was 'Yes, thanks!' After six months of this, he couldn't wait to give the monk a piece of his mind. He returned to the monastery and found the monk waiting for him.

"That was the most ridiculous thing I've ever done!" growled the villager. "It was a complete waste of time! That's the last time I ever come to you for advice."

The monk smiled at the villager. "Yes, thanks!" he said.

The villager stared at the monk incredulously and felt his anger rising inside him. Then, as he was about to lash out at the monk one more time, he felt his anger disappear, and he had what the monks call a "sudden insight." He understood that he had a choice in what happened next.

The two of them stared at each other, the air electric between them. "I just have one final thing to say to you," the villager said. Then he bowed deeply to the monk and said, "Yes, thanks!" With that, he and the monk embraced each other, and they laughed so hard that tears came into their eyes.

When your life is going gently down the stream and you can surrender to the fact that you cannot really control the entire course of your life, then you can open yourself to a life of surprises. You can embrace the beauty of life's uncertainty. You can have the basic trust to say, "Yes, thanks!" to whatever unexpected things may float your way.

SIXTEEN

What Would Water Do?

Water is fluid, soft, and yielding. But water will wear
away rock, which is rigid and cannot yield.

—Lao-tzu

A S MY UNCLE Joe started to get on in years, whenever he invited me to go camping with him I tried to re-arrange my schedule so I could make it happen. Uncle Joe was always a wise counselor, and being out in the woods with him was an exceptional opportunity for learning.

The very last time we went camping together was among the most special. As the day progressed, we wound up hiking much farther than was comfortable for my uncle, since he was nearing eighty years of age. I noticed that his breath was becoming labored, so we decided to sit and rest.

He walked over to a lovely brook that was trickling through

the woods and downward to a small pool, which became a small waterfall just below where we stopped. I found a rock that was rather flattened on the top and sat down near him.

"Let's just relax here for a while," he said, "and you can catch your breath. We'll see what wisdom we can take from watching the water."

I smiled at the thought that he was stopping so that I could catch my breath. "What are you talking about?" I asked.

"Let's stop talking for a while and just watch the water."

I started to object but my uncle just snorted out a quick, "Trust me!"

We must have sat there in silence watching the stream for at least fifteen or twenty minutes. Then Uncle Joe broke the silence. "So, what do you notice?"

"It's quiet. It's beautiful here. I feel peaceful."

"Yes, that's true, but what do you notice about the water?"

"Nothing in particular. The water is just part of the beauty. What am I supposed to notice about it? Okay, the water here is very clean and clear. Is that what you want me to notice?"

"It's fine to notice all of those things," he said softly, "but notice also that the water doesn't struggle, it just flows. When it is confronted by an obstacle like that rock over there, the water doesn't get upset or aggressive, it just flows around the rock. If we could sit here long enough, we would notice that the water eventually would wear down the rock."

We were both silent for a long time again, as I thought about what Uncle Joe was telling me. "The Eastern philosophers have a saying," he continued, " 'You can't catch running water in a bucket.' The idea is that if you try to capture the running water in the bucket you will end up with standing water. The only way to have running water is to be willing to let it go. Sometimes in life we have to let go in order to have what we really want."

I knew that my uncle was teaching me something that I needed to learn and apply in my life. Letting go of the negative was never easy for me.

He continued, "Whenever I find myself in stressful, difficult, negative situations, I ask myself, What would water do? It helps remind me to flow instead of struggle.

"Stressful situations are not necessarily what they seem. The best way to survive any so-called stressful situation is to keep remembering that whatever is happening in your life, you always have a choice to struggle or to flow. Once you remember that, you can relax and ask yourself, What is the learning here for me? and What would water do? If you can learn something from whatever happens to you, things will seem very different in your life."

So many times throughout my life I have called upon the wisdom that my uncle Joe imparted to me on that last camping trip. Over the years I have often been faced with negative situations, at work and in virtually every other aspect of my daily life.

For example, a few years back I almost became involved in a road rage incident. I was driving on a three-lane road and—not seeing anyone coming—moved from the right lane into the middle lane. Suddenly, I noticed that another driver, approaching rapidly from behind, was switching from the left lane into the middle lane right beside me.

We barely missed crashing together, but were able to swerve back into our original lanes. The man in the other car slowed so that he could scream and shake his fist at me. Then his fist uncoiled into a single middle finger as he sped off.

I began to fume, and defended my driving to myself. "It was no more my fault than his!" Then, in my anger, I was able to make it even more his fault than mine: "At least *I* was going the speed limit!" Finally, I dismissed him with one savage word, identifying his whole person with an orifice usually held in high esteem by proctologists.

As fate would have it, he had sped away only to catch the next red light, so he was sitting at the intersection when I pulled up beside him. He was still red-faced with anger. He quickly lowered his electric window on the passenger side and—once again—yelled some further abuse at me. "You're an idiot!"

My initial thought was to respond, *"I am not an idiot! You're the idiot!"* My next thought was to escalate the situation considerably by crawling through his open window to choke him within an inch of his life! At that moment, I remembered my uncle's simple advice. I asked myself, "Do I really want to start a fight with this jerk? What would water do? How can I just flow with this situation, instead?"

In a sudden flash of inspiration, I simply smiled and said to the man in a calm and thoughtful voice, "You know that's interesting because I was just thinking the same thing. I *am* an idiot!" I could tell that my response had totally undone him, for he was speechless, and his face showed it. He was clearly struggling now with how to respond and could think of nothing to say.

At last, he broke into a grin. He gave a little friendly wave and drove away. I smiled, too. I knew that a situation that could have been very nasty and, at the very least, a negative experience that would have haunted me throughout the day had been transformed into something quite different.

I have enjoyed telling this story to other people many times. For some reason, I imagine that he has told it even more times than I have! In addition to bringing joy instead of suffering to us both, I had a powerful lesson reinforced. As Uncle Joe taught me many years ago, we always have a choice in life. We can get caught up in the negative and suffer the consequences. Or we can choose to go gently down the stream. Successful people make a habit of the latter.

SEVENTEEN

See Things as They Are

People are not disturbed by things, but by the view they take of them.

—EPICTETUS

OUR IDEAS ABOUT the way things should be often bring us stress and anxiety. When we discover something quite contrary to what we expect, we have a difficult time flowing with the new reality we have discovered.

One of my friends and colleagues has a sign in his office that reads, "Since I gave up all hope, I feel so much better!" Disappointments create so much stress and unhappiness in our lives that keeping our expectations low may seem like a good idea. On the other hand, it is also true that it is important for us to have extraordinarily high goals and to envision great possibilities for our success. Like so many things in life, wisdom is often found in finding a way to balance opposites. As the old

English proverb has it, "Hope for the best and prepare for the worst."

The problem is not that we have expectations. Expectations are one way that we organize our experience and create a life that is not chaotic. Having an image about what our future success looks like is a good step toward making our dreams a reality. The problem occurs when we become inflexible and rigid about our expectations. We need to develop the capacity to flow like water when those expectations don't become real. How much easier would our lives be if we could just back off a little from our rigid expectations of other people, for example? How much more gently could we flow through our lives if we had fewer assumptions about how things should or could be?

The wise Stoic philosopher Epictetus taught that when we go about any action whatsoever, we should always be keenly aware of the nature of that action. For example, he wrote about going to the public baths in ancient Rome, "If you are going to bathe, picture to yourself the things which usually happen in the bath: some people splash the water, some push, some use abusive language, and others steal. Thus you will more safely go about this action if you say to yourself, 'I will now go bathe and keep my own mind in a state conformable to nature.'" We might have to update Epictetus's insight to a visit to the mall or a drive to work through heavy traffic, but you get the idea.

Having unrealistic expectations about the nature of the world can make us miserable, keeping us from the success and happiness that we want. As a service to you, I offer for your consideration a list of things I have learned are a part of the natural way of reality. If you find yourself expecting life to be otherwise, then you can't say that you weren't warned in advance.

- *Things change.* As the philosopher Heraclitus had it, the only thing that doesn't change is change itself.

Things won't be like they were when you were growing up. For that matter things won't be like they were yesterday. People change, too, but not on your timetable.

- *Things break.* The toilet will overflow and the car won't start. New things break, too. Your favorite things break. Computer files disappear. Bodies break and hearts break, too. Things can be fixed, but not always. Sometimes they stay broken.

- *People will let you down.* Coworkers will try to undo your best efforts. People you trust will betray you. Friends and family members will disappoint you. You are a person, so you will also let yourself down.

- *People will lie and break promises.* There will be gossip about you that is unfair. People won't show up to repair the toilet or fix the car when they said they would. You will forgive someone, and then they will hurt you again.

- *Things get stolen and lost.* Your favorite things included. Your expensive things will be stolen or lost. Things no one but you could use or value will be stolen or lost. You will find only one sock of the pair in the dryer. People will hang up just when you get to the phone. Loss happens all the time.

- *You will discover incompetence.* Customer service will treat you like you are Osama bin Laden. Doctors will leave the scalpel in your abdomen. The person at the information booth won't know a thing.

- *Results won't be instant.* Things take time. You will be told otherwise (see "People will lie," above.) Rapid transit won't be. Weight will come off at least as slowly as you put it on. Teenagers will be teenagers for seven years if they live that long.

- *Fruit ripens.* People will reap what they sow. What goes around comes around. Not only will results not be instant, you may not even be able to see them. You are not exempt from the laws of nature. Your actions will follow you, as well.

- *Sometimes bad things will happen to good people.* Things won't always be fair. Sometimes the good will suffer and the wicked will prosper. Sometimes the very worst will happen to the very best and vice versa.

- *The world will not be logical or safe.* The telephone store will have an unlisted number. You will be required to follow rules that make absolutely no sense. People will make decisions that affect your safety who shouldn't be making those decisions.

If all this appears somewhat negative and cynical, then let me hasten to add that I believe the nature of things is also enormously positive, and in my own life I want to focus on the positive. However, when we realize that we cannot exercise control over many of the people and things that influence our lives, then we can relax and be more flexible. When we can let go of trying to control those things that are really outside of our control, then we can choose a path that makes our lives better and less stressful. Only then can we truly flow gently down the stream.

EIGHTEEN

The Miracle of Breath

Whine less, breathe more.

—SWEDISH PROVERB

A S A SMALL boy, when I would be awakened by a nightmare, a scary noise, or some other event that would bring on middle-of-the-night thoughts of the boogeyman, I would fearfully leave my bed and sneak into my parents' bedroom. I was not permitted to crawl into their bed, so I would with great stealth crawl to my mother's side of the bed and then lie down on the floor.

I discovered that my fear would vanish when I listened to my mother's deep breathing. I can still recall her long, slow, deep inhalation, followed by an ever so brief pause. Then, her equally unhurried exhalation followed peacefully. I was almost instantly put at ease. The fear would disappear. Peace and calm would replace any emotional upset, and sleep would come to me there on the floor.

Many years later, I was taught much more about the remarkably transformative qualities of the breath by Vietnamese Zen master Thich Nhat Hanh. He taught that with a few simple breaths we can bring much peace and happiness into our lives. We can simply turn our attention to our breathing, and as we breathe in we say silently to ourselves, *calming*. Then, as we pay close attention to our exhale we say, *smiling*, and bring a small smile to our lips.

After following our breath like that for no more than five minutes, we will discover that we feel nourished. We feel peaceful and calm. Of course, if we are very agitated and upset when we decide to calm ourselves with this marvelous practice, then it may require that we breathe like that for somewhat longer.

One of the things that I so love about this practice, in addition to its unbelievable simplicity, is that it is completely portable. We can practice using our breath to make ourselves calm anywhere, and no one will even know! It is like possessing a powerful secret potion. If we are in a very contentious meeting at work, then without saying a word we can make ourselves peaceful, while everyone around us is going crazy.

Calming. Smiling.

Calming. Smiling.

If we are in the middle of a traffic jam, and we start to feel our frustration and anger rising, then we have a solution.

Calming, Smiling.

Calming. Smiling.

My wife and I very rarely quarrel anymore, and when we do, it doesn't last very long. We both are determined to take responsibility for our actions, and one or the other of us will usually put an end to the argument before it can rage out of control. I attribute much of my own progress in this regard to the fact that I have learned the three magical phrases. No, not the three magic words, although uttering "I love you" in the midst of a round of bickering is an excellent idea as well.

The three magical phrases are: "I'm sorry." "I was wrong." "It was entirely my fault." I have found that these phrases, strung together just so, with a genuine level of sincerity, will put a halt to any dispute we may have. Of course, before I could experience the wondrous power of these three phrases, it was necessary to discover the beauty of "letting go of being right"—discussion of which I will save for another time.

As it plays out now, my wife and I will start to bicker over some insignificant matter. (Aren't the vast majority of all disputes between couples rather inconsequential in retrospect?) As soon as I remember to bring forth the magical phrases, I utter them. My wife then smiles, says "thank you, dearest," the quarrel is over, and we peacefully and happily get on with our lives.

The last time my wife and I had a really bad disagreement, it took me a while before I had the presence of mind to remember that I was in possession of a wealth of magic. Fortunately, before the quarrel escalated out of control, I remembered to put my mind on my breathing.

Calming. Smiling.
Calming. Smiling.

After a few moments of following my breath in this way, I was able to remember the three magical phrases. I calmly looked at my wife and said, "I'm sorry. I was wrong. It was entirely my fault."

We both stopped in the middle of the argument, and there was a pregnant pause. My wife, still a bit miffed, said in an accusing voice, "You've been breathing again!" This observation was followed by yet another pregnant pause before we both realized how funny it was. We both began to laugh out loud. It is exceedingly difficult for a fight to continue when both parties are also involved in belly laughs.

In recent years, I have expanded the manner in which I practice the miracle of breath. This slight change has even further enhanced my capacity to be peaceful and happy in even the most difficult situations. I share this modified version with you so that you might go even more gently down the stream. As I breathe in, I silently say to myself, *gently*. As I breathe out, I say, *flowing*.

Gently. Flowing.
Gently. Flowing.

NINETEEN

Pig Wrestling

A long dispute means that both parties are wrong.

—VOLTAIRE

WHENEVER I WOULD get caught up in recounting some power struggle that I was involved in, my uncle Joe would invariably offer up his favorite injunction: "Son, never wrestle with a pig. You both get dirty, and the pig loves it!" After too many years of experience, I have realized that Uncle Joe's down-home wisdom was not just funny; it was also great advice for anyone interested in going gently down the stream.

Uncle Joe's advice, I have grown to understand, is not just about realizing that you should avoid engaging with someone who is acting like a pig. The real learning is more about self-knowledge and awareness; that is, when you start to wrestle with a pig, you become piggy yourself. A major step to walking the path of peace is to recognize your own lack of skillfulness by becoming engaged in the conflict in the first place.

Struggling, quarreling, bickering, and blaming are never the path to peace. Yes, it is true that calm often follows the storm; however, it is a mistake of both logical and meteorological proportions to infer that the calm was caused by the storm. Furthermore, whenever we start to believe that our disputes and power struggles are entirely the fault of the other person and not ourselves, it is time to remember another of Uncle Joe's favorite proverbs—"It takes two to tango."

In the previous chapter I discussed the power of the three magical phrases: "I'm sorry." "I was wrong." "It was entirely my fault." When I have shared these three magical phrases with other people, I often hear this concern: "But this is just one person taking the blame! What about the other person? Surely it's not *always* entirely your fault!" These questions show a lack of awareness about the profound nature of pig wrestling—it does, indeed, take two to tangle.

Seen in this light it is easy to see why it is appropriate to begin with "I'm sorry." I apologize for my own lack of skill in participating in this conflict. I am sorry that I got into pig wrestling. So, too, "I was wrong." In other words, I made a mistake. It was a mistake for me to behave in ways that contributed to this unproductive, dirty, and muddy struggle. It was a mistake for me to join in the wrestling. Finally, "It was entirely my fault." This is an acknowledgment that without my unskillful participation, this bout of pig wrestling could not have occurred. That is obviously the truth. So, "It was entirely my fault" is merely about taking personal responsibility for my own actions.

None of this is meant to suggest that our fellow pig-wrestler may not also have been at fault, as well. That is more than likely the case. However, if I take it as my calling to try to force the other person to see his or her unskillful conduct, then I am really not serious about bringing peace and calm to my life. No one has ever argued anyone else into self-awareness about his or her own unskillful behavior.

All I can do is to take responsibility for my own actions, not try to change someone else's. If I am sincere about going gently down the stream, then I have to become the very peacefulness that I want. As Uncle Joe's maxim clearly teaches, pig wrestling leads to both people getting dirty. As we move through life, we do not want to wallow along all covered with dirt, even if the people we care about are pulling at us to join them in the mud. Rather, we want to show them that there is another way to live, as we flow gently in the cleansing waters of the stream.

TWENTY

Let It Go

No human condition is ever permanent.

—SOCRATES

A FEW YEARS AGO my daughter, who had recently graduated from college and was having some difficulty finding work in her chosen field—English literature— decided to take a position with Delta Airlines while she worked on her master's degree. I was happy to learn that she was gainfully employed and even happier to learn that it meant that I would become immediately eligible for a free round-trip ticket anywhere in the United States.

My wife and I were planning a romantic week-long getaway to Seattle and the San Juan Islands, so I suggested that she use her frequent flyer miles and I would use the free ticket. Of course, this meant I would be flying standby, but my daughter told me that it shouldn't be much of a problem if we chose our flights carefully. So my wife booked her reward flights, and we chose the worst possible hours for the trip, assuming that would likely ensure my standby ticket would work.

I often fly in my comfort clothes—T-shirt, shorts, and sandals—so my daughter warned me that I should wear "decent business clothes" or the gate agent might not let me board. When we eagerly arrived at the airport for our scheduled flight to Seattle, I wore my "concession clothes"—a sports jacket, a nice tie, and my best pair of designer jeans.

When I checked in with the gate agent, she told me to have a seat in the waiting area and she would call me as soon as she could be sure that I could get on as a standby passenger.

I hadn't been sitting for more than two or three minutes when the agent called my name. I went to the counter and she said, "No problem. I can go ahead and give you a boarding pass for first class." For about a microsecond I had a small moral dilemma. I knew that if I flew first class I could not sit with my wife, who already had a seat assignment in coach. "That will be great!" I said. Then I walked back over with my boarding pass and explained to my wife very simply, "They just put me in first class, what could I do?"

I could tell that my wife was not all that excited about the long flight alone in coach with her snack meal. The fact that I was enjoying a lovely dinner in first class did not exactly add to her thrill factor. My midflight gift delivery to her of my chocolate mousse dessert drew nothing but a rather curt, "No, thanks, I've already had nuts." Once we landed all was soon forgiven, however, and we had a lovely, romantic week of vacation.

We had booked my wife's return flight with a 12:01 A.M. departure from Seattle, thinking that the flight would likely have room for standby passengers like me. We arrived at the gate about an hour before the flight, and the gate agent, once again, told me to have a seat and she would call me if she could get me on the flight. As before, I had not been seated more than two or three minutes when the agent called my name.

I went to the counter and the gate agent said in a noticeably cold tone, "Sir, you are wearing jeans." I was, at first, simply perplexed by her comment. I was wearing my same flying outfit of sports coat, nice shirt with tie, and fancy jeans, and I couldn't imagine why she was commenting on my jeans. Then for some reason it occurred to me that perhaps there was some problem with putting me in first class wearing jeans. So I reassured her, "Oh, no problem, I can just ride in coach. I know the airplane is not full, so maybe you can put my wife and me together in coach."

In the next instant, I realized that things had taken a turn for the worse. The gate agent responded in an even nastier tone laced with mock politeness, "You don't understand, *sir*. You aren't flying first class or any other class. I can't let you board the airplane in jeans. Company policy says when family fly on free passes they have to dress in business attire, and jeans aren't business attire." I protested that I had flown out to Seattle in the very same clothes and that I had been given a seat in first class. She very curtly replied, "Then they violated company policy, *sir*, which I don't plan to do!" Then with one word, she cut off all further conversation, "Period!"

My wife, sensing that there was some problem, had arrived by my side as the gate agent turned to help another customer. I explained the problem to my wife and we considered our plight— our luggage was already checked, no stores were open in the airport at that hour, and the plane was scheduled for departure in less than a half hour. We both had important meetings at home the next day, to boot. We had to get on that flight!

My wife then stepped back to the counter and surprised me with her question to the agent. "What if he puts on my pants? Could he get on the plane then?"

The agent peered over the counter to glance at my wife's sleek black slacks and then said, "The policy doesn't say that the pants have to fit," and then turned away.

We took that as a yes, but I started to protest to my wife. "I can't wear your pants! I'm seven inches taller than you are, and my waist has got to be at least seven or eight inches bigger!"

My wife simply looked at me and repeated, "We have to get on that flight."

So off we went in the Seattle airport looking for a place to switch pants. Obviously, the restrooms were out. We finally found an empty gate where we huddled and hid as best we could behind the abandoned ticket counter and made the switch. Frankly, my wife looked almost stylish and somewhat cool in my jeans—pant legs rolled up, jeans billowing a bit at the waist from the tightened belt. I, on the other hand, looked very strange and—I imagined— like someone who might scare the other passengers.

We arrived back at the now deserted gate for our flight and my wife presented me to the agent with only five minutes until the scheduled departure. The gate agent walked around from behind the counter and looked me up and down like a drill sergeant inspecting a new recruit. I could not even begin to zip the slacks, so I was holding my briefcase in front of me to avoid exposing myself. All three buttons of my sports coat were buttoned to provide as much coverage as possible. The agent paused in her inspection at my ankles. There were at least four inches of bare leg exposed above my socks! I have never before or since felt or looked as ridiculous. "Fine!" she said gruffly. Then she walked back around the counter and, without another word, issued me a boarding pass—for the very last row in coach.

My wife, who had a seat near the front of the cabin, had assured me that once we were airborne we could figure out a way to switch pants "after they turn off the lights." I knew that would be a while, so I just sat and wallowed in my misery, sweating bullets. Soon we took off, and after what seemed like an eternity the captain turned off the lights so that passengers on this red-eye flight could sleep. Shortly thereafter my wife came back and told me that she had explained our situation to her seatmate, who thought that the whole affair was both outrageous and hilarious. My wife told me that she would use a blanket to take off my jeans at her seat. I could then come get the jeans and go to the restroom, make the switch, and bring her pants to her.

After what seemed like an eternity, we both were back in our rightful pants. I took the vacant seat on the aisle just across from my wife. I kept leaning over to her and saying things like, "Can you believe this happened? What was the deal with that hateful gate agent?"

I was fuming, but my wife was just laughing. She kept making little jokes like, "Delta is ready when your pants are!" She thought the whole thing was very funny. I, on the other hand, was so humiliated and upset that I couldn't see any humor at all. All I could think about was how to get revenge on my tormentor, the wicked gate agent.

Finally, my wife said, "Listen, I've heard you in speech after speech tell people to learn the art of transforming negative experiences in their lives. You tell them not to get stuck in the negative. That's exactly what you are doing. So get over it! Let it go! Find a way to reframe this situation so it won't drive you crazy. Find a way that you can look at it that is fun!"

Of course, I instantly realized that my wife was spot-on. The more I focused on the negative experience, the more unhappy I was making myself. The more I continued to think about the past, which was something over which I had no control, the more I was adding to my present misery. Not to mention the fact that all my revenge fantasies were having no effect at all on the gate agent. I began to soothe myself with the much more philosophical idea of people reaping what they sow. I told myself that if the universe were just, then she would have her own misery to reap one day. I, on the other hand, was only bringing misery on myself. I needed to let it go.

So I tried to practice what I preach. I began to breathe slowly to calm myself down. I breathed like that for several minutes. Then I asked myself, "Okay, what's another way that I can look at this situation so that it won't make me angry and upset? What's a way that I can hold this experience so that it is joyful rather than crazy making? What's another version of reality that can help to put this behind me?" I sat like that for about ten minutes, but nothing came to me. I like to think of myself as a creative type, but I was drawing a blank. My anger with the gate agent continued to block all creativity.

I leaned across the aisle and nudged my wife, who was peacefully trying to doze. "I need a little help here," I said. "Nothing fun is coming to me. The negative thoughts keep creeping in."

"Now you're starting to annoy me!" she said, and I could tell she was only half joking. Then she sat up in her seat and said, "All right, I just thought of something."

"Let's have it!" I said eagerly.

"Okay," she said. "Think of it this way: just how often will a young woman like that gate agent help a man your age get into another woman's pants?" With this she let out a little cackle of laughter, and for the first time in hours I was able to laugh with her.

With a smile on her face my wife pulled the blanket up to her chin and closed her eyes. I leaned back in my seat and smiled, too.

I immediately noticed how much better I felt. I wasn't sleepy, so I started to think about ways that I could remember in the future that getting caught up in the negative and entertaining painful thoughts do nothing but sabotage my own happiness.

We always have choices, and I was certain that I did not want to continue making the choice of stress and negativity. I was sure that I wanted to begin making the choice for happiness from then on. So as we winged our way home, I thought of several questions that I could ask myself each time I was being carried along by negative thinking.

What is a way that I can look at this situation that will bring me joy instead of stress?

How can I make myself smile about this situation right now?

If I can't make myself smile about it, whom do I know who can help me?

How can I put this behind me in a positive and life-affirming way?

How can I let it go?

You may want to consider these questions at times when you are stuck in the negative, too. Do you have a burning problem in your life right now? Negative situations are called "burning problems" for a good reason—if you hold on to them too tightly, you're sure to get burned. When holding tightly to that burning problem begins to cause you pain, the best thing you can do is to just let it go.

PART III

MERRILY, MERRILY, MERRILY, MERRILY

*People who are successful laugh and play at
least four times as much as most people. If you
want to be successful in life , then you must bring
more laughter, play, and fun into your life.
Your life will become more joyful,
productive, and successful.*

TWENTY-ONE

Lighten Up!

The most wasted of all days is one without laughter.

—E. E. CUMMINGS

T HE TRIBAL WISDOM of the Lakota Indians says, "When you discover that you are riding a dead horse, it is a good time to dismount." Many of us suffer from a disease that I call "terminal seriousness." Most people who suffer from this malady are not even aware that they have an ailment. They simply go through life with the grim determination to, well, just get through it. Then they do. It should surprise no one that a synonym for serious is grave.

If we are truly sincere about wanting to live a life of genuine success, then it is high time to realize that terminal seriousness is a dead horse, and right now is a good time to dismount.

Unfortunately, many of us continue to ride that dead horse. We are killing ourselves with seriousness. When I say we are "killing ourselves," I mean that quite literally. People who take themselves too seriously are very likely to wind up seriously ill. How do I know for certain that our ability to lighten up will enormously influence our opportunities for success? From years of research and investigation (although admittedly without firsthand experience) I have concluded that it is exceedingly difficult for dead people to be successful.

We have all heard the old saw "Laughter is the best medicine." Most often this is understood as merely saying that laughter is good for our emotional state. In reality, however, overwhelming research clearly shows that people who laugh and play more are not only happier but also physically healthier. More laughter and play in our lives will do wonders for our immune system, lower our stress levels (with the corresponding health benefits of lower stress), and help us to heal more quickly from stress-related illnesses.

Recent research even shows that laughter can help you lose weight! Researchers at Vanderbilt University determined that people who are laughing are burning 20 percent more calories than people who are standing around with a serious look on their faces. The researchers calculated that people who laugh for ten to fifteen minutes a day could lose more than four pounds every year!

This, of course, should be reason enough for most of us to learn the wisdom of frequent and hearty laughter. However, there is more that laughter can do to contribute to our success. Evidence also shows that people who laugh more are more creative, better team players, and much more productive. So we have every reason not to take ourselves so seriously, to laugh as often as possible, and—in general—to lighten up.

If you wonder if you may be suffering from terminal seriousness, then there are a few helpful questions you can ask yourself.

How playful or how serious am I in a typical day?

In what situations does the spirit of play and fun emerge in my life?

In what situations am I nearly always serious?

In what situations am I comfortable laughing and playing?

Am I able to laugh at myself?

Perhaps after answering these questions you will be able to better diagnose your own situation. If you are suffering from terminal seriousness, then fortunately there is a simple treatment— you need to make it a priority to bring more laughter into your life. Once you do this on a regular basis, then you will be able to enjoy the wonderful benefits of dismounting from the dead horse of seriousness.

TWENTY-TWO

The Antidote for Terminal Seriousness

*The wit makes fun of other persons; the satirist of
the world; the humorist of himself.*

—JAMES THURBER

WHEN SOMETHING EMBARRASSING happens to us, most people want to forget about it as soon as possible and move on to something else. However, those times in our lives when we have made a laughingstock of ourselves can actually be of great value as a reminder not to take ourselves too seriously. We all have those times—both big and small—when we have embarrassed ourselves in front of other people. Instead of being ashamed of those times, we can treasure them and wear them proudly. When we start to take ourselves a bit too seriously, we can recall those instances to remind us to lighten up. If you want to reap all the benefits of a life of merriment, the first step is to learn to laugh at yourself.

Just the other day, for example, I had the opportunity to meet Steve Nash, who had just been named Most Valuable Player in the National Basketball Association. Steve is Canadian, and he is only the second foreign-born athlete to win the M.V.P. award. I congratulated him on his fine accomplishment and then, trying to make conversation, I said, "I'm going to be spending the entire summer up in your neck of the woods. For the next four months I'm going to be living in Vancouver."

He politely asked where I would be staying.

I said, "Oh, I have rented a house very near USB." He gave me a puzzled look, so I quickly added, "Very close to the port."

Not that this explanation had helped at all, but his eyes suddenly lit up with recognition and he said, "Oh, you mean UBC . . . the University of British Columbia." Then, after another pause, he added, "On the bay."

I allowed that this was, of course, what I meant—UBC. On the bay. Of course I didn't mean USB—and why did I say port? We continued to make small talk, but in the back of my mind I was constantly worrying, "How could I have been so stupid? What was I thinking with 'USB' and 'the port'?"

We parted for the evening, and as I drove away it hit me that a USB was in fact a place on my computer where I hooked up various devices, and it was, indeed, called a USB "port." I started to laugh at my own mistake. Then I laughed even more at my having been so concerned about such a silly slipup in the first place. Why had I spent even a moment torturing myself over something so unimportant? Did Steve Nash really care?

I laughed once again when I got home and Googled "USB." I figured that I might as well know what sorts of things were tumbling around in my fertile and not-so-organized brain. I learned that USB stands for Universal Service Bus. Once I started treading lightly about my faux pas, I found everything about it extremely humorous. After all, I had just told Steve Nash that I was going to be living near a Universal Service Bus. Perhaps I could invite him to ride the bus to work with me someday!

At this point, I decided to check out USB in the Universal Acronym Finder and things got even funnier. It turns out that USB also stands for "Upflow Sludge Bed." That sounded like quite a nice neighborhood to rent a place for the summer! So I laughed some more. My favorite of the dozen or so acronyms that the Acronym Finder offered for USB was "Usama Bin Laden." I had a good laugh over that one, too. "Yes, Steve, I'll be living in Vancouver near Usama Bin Laden! Maybe you will want to come up for a visit. Bring the twins along!"

The point, of course, is that if we can remember to lighten up and not take ourselves so seriously, we can open up all sorts of doors to laughter, play, and joy in our lives. As far as I know, this is the only antidote for terminal seriousness.

TWENTY-THREE

Have Fun at Work

A sense of humor is a part of the art of leadership, of getting along with people, of getting things done.

—DWIGHT D. EISENHOWER

CONVENTIONAL BUSINESS WISDOM says that work is not supposed to be fun . . . that's why it's called "work"! Many examples in this book demonstrate that, in fact, the opposite is true. Among the numerous benefits to having fun at work is that employee stress levels decrease and there is a corresponding increase in morale, creativity, and productivity. Best of all there's an increase in customer satisfaction because the true secret of fun at work is that people like to do business with people who *like* to do business. Fun at work is like a magnet to draw in new business and to form long-term relationships with your best customers.

If I'm your customer, then of course I'm going to choose a business relationship with my head. I'm interested in value, in service, and in costs. But I'm also going to choose with my gut. How do I *feel* doing business with your company? An organization whose employees have a positive attitude—who feel rewarded, recognized, appreciated, and who happily greet their customers— is an organization that has discovered a key element to forming long-term customer relationships.

Many companies have learned the value of fun at work, and yours can, too. If you look in Chase's Official Calendar of Events, you will see that April 1 has been officially designated "International Fun at Work Day." There is always strength in numbers, so an easy way to get started is to join with thousands of other organizations across the globe that are celebrating International Fun at Work Day along with you!

Each year Playfair, Inc., the founder of Fun at Work Day, suggests a theme for that year's celebration. For example, the Sixth Annual Fun at Work Day was entitled "Let's Do Lunch!" Playfair invited everyone to "pull up a chair, lift up a fork, and dig into a delicious company lunch to celebrate Fun at Work Day." This was its sample "Menu of Ideas":

- Treat the entire company to lunch and have the officers of the company serve the food.

- Ask your competitor over for lunch or invite your vendors to your potluck.

- Guess who made what? Anonymously put all the potluck dishes on a table. Place a large number by each item. Pass out paper with numbers on it. Have everyone try to guess who made each dish. The one with the most correct answers is first in line to be served for the feast!

- Invite a local chef to your company for a demonstration during lunch about "fast meals for busy professionals."

- Have two departments in your company meet for lunch. (Each department can be responsible for different parts of the meal.)

- Have everyone bring a dish with a personal story associated with it—an ethnic specialty, your kids' favorite, your grandmother's specialty. Share your stories.

What if you work for a company that simply doesn't value fun at work? In fact, you may work for an organization that suffers from a severe case of terminal seriousness. In that case, you will need to empower yourself to become one of the organizational innovators.

In the "diffusion of innovation" theory (also known as the "multistep flow" theory, which is quite appropriate for a book about flowing "gently down the stream"), Everett Rogers notes that trying to convince a large mass of people to embrace a controversial innovation is a waste of time. To be a successful innovator, you must work with the small number of other innovators and the "early adopters."

So if you work for a company that doesn't appreciate fun at work, begin with the people in your organization who—like you—are fun-loving and playful people. Before long you will be leading an "early majority" into the great benefits of fun at work. Before you can say "Happy Fun at Work Day," you will be wondering why that small group of "laggards" are left behind and still wallowing in terminal seriousness.

If you think it is difficult to be the person who brings Fun at Work Day to your company, then think of Sigurthor Gunnlaugsson, marketing director of the Kringlan Shopping Center, who set himself an even loftier goal—to bring Fun at Work Day to his entire country!

"You can now add Iceland to the 'Fun at Work Day,'" proclaimed Sigurthor proudly. "What I did here in the Kringlan Shopping Center management office was to ask everyone at the office to bring in their favorite hat. Then I asked them to take pictures of themselves and their hat with a digital camera. Then I posted all the pictures on the computer and asked the employees to vote on which hat belonged to which person.

"During the coffee break in the afternoon I brought in a cake which looked like a cowboy hat with candles on it, which formed the shape of 'K,' the first letter in our company name. Then we had a little ceremony, like at the Oscars, and the winner was awarded a big Easter egg made of chocolate. It was a lot of fun! I'm already sending out your newsletter to many of my marketing colleagues to make April 1 next year a 'Fun at Work Day' in all of Iceland."

If one person can be the innovator who brings fun at work to his entire country, then surely you can change your organization. Be bold! Start today.

TWENTY-FOUR

Laugh Out Loud

*I was irrevocably betrothed to laughter, the sound
of which has always seemed to me to be the most
civilized music in the world.*

—PETER USTINOV

RECENTLY MY WIFE started having much more on-
line interaction with her students in internet discussions.
The other day she sent me an email asking, "What is
LOL?" For some reason the question made me, well, laugh out
loud. I suppose my own laughter was brought about by remembering some of the internet and chat abbreviations that I have read
over the years.

I wrote back and told her that LOL meant "laughing out
loud," and that her question had me ROTFL, "rolling on the floor
laughing." Our internet friends, however, are not just laughing
out loud, rolling on the floor laughing, or anything so staid. They

are LSHIBAMF, "laughing so hard I broke all my furniture," and LSHIHTCMS, "laughing so hard I had to change my shorts!" Perhaps none are laughing as hysterically as those who are ROT-FLMAOWPIMP, "rolling on the floor laughing my ass off while peeing in my pants!"

As someone who has spent most of a career extolling the virtues of laughter and play, I must say that I appreciate the attitude almost as much as the visual images. On the other hand, I suspect that these internet communicators may be actually involved in a bit of ED—"electronic deception." I've read some pretty hilarious things on the internet, but in all cases my furniture has been safe from destruction and my pants have stayed clean and dry. I do believe that all of us very much need to laugh out loud as often as we can. We should not, however, simply sit at our computers, in our offices, or in front of the television just waiting for it to happen. We need to become intentional about our laughter.

When you become intentional about bringing more laughter into your life, you discover that the world is actually a very funny place in which to live. If you are looking for the humorous, then you will find it everywhere. Just this past week, for example, I saw a sign on an electrical repair truck that said, "Let Us Remove Your Shorts!" I also saw a sign at the dry cleaning store that had the simple command, "Drop Your Pants Here!"

Laughter is good for our mental and physical well-being, so—like other things that are good for us—we should take heavy doses of this wonderful elixir. More and more organizations are now taking laughter very seriously. Dru Bookout, a faculty member at Richland College, has as one of her assigned duties the scheduling of regular "Laugh Breaks" for the college community. The entire campus is notified in advance of the time and place for this fifteen-minute hilarity gathering. When employees arrive for their break,

Dru provides a comedy video, a game, an open microphone for bad jokes, or some other laughter-producing activity. Shortly thereafter everyone returns to work feeling energized from the shared fun.

Jim Mann works in technical support at CompuCom Systems, a company that provides IT support to corporate users for everything from Microsoft Office products to BlackBerry wireless devices. Recently, Jim told me about the latest celebration of "Customer Service Week," which his company holds as a way to thank its employees for providing great customer service. All during the week employees were able to participate in fun events like paper airplane engineering competitions, cubicle decorating contests, chili and dessert cooking fêtes, and radio-controlled car races. "It was a great week with lots of laughter," Jim recalled. "Laughing together was such a great way to reduce stress around the office, and that good feeling carried right over into the next week."

So wherever we find ourselves—at home, at the office, in our cars, and, of course, sitting at our computers—we can look for opportunities to laugh out loud. We can make it a daily intention in our lives. Who knows, with enough practice we may even end up laughing so hard that we break all the furniture. LSHIBAMF forever!

TWENTY-FIVE

A Merry Heart

*Happiness is not an individual matter. When you are able
to bring relief or bring back the smile to one person, not
only that person profits, but you also profit.*

—THICH NHAT HANH

THE BOOK OF Proverbs tells us that "a merry heart
doeth good like medicine." It is important to remember
the connection between being merry and having an open
heart. If we want to travel merrily through life, then we need to
pay attention to the teachings of our heart. When we are coming
from a place of caring and service to others, when we treat the
people we encounter from a place of openheartedness and love,
then merriment cannot be far behind. Of course we always want to
approach our families and our friends from a place of love; however, even situations at work can provide an opportunity to lead
with the heart.

Kelly Eaves works in the IT department at the Voluntary Hospital Association in Dallas. One summer Kelly took his family to the Florida Keys for a lobster fishing vacation. When Kelly returned to work on the Monday after his vacation, he found his office cubicle had been completely transformed into a tropical hut. While he was away, his team members had totally covered the outside of his office with bamboo fencing. One of the guys on his team was a gardener, and he had put tomato stakes and baling wire across the top of the cubicle to support a roof made of bamboo mats. Grass skirts were unraveled into long strands of grass hanging down from the roof.

Tiki torches were wired to the outside of the hut, and multicolored leis and coconut bras were hanging over the sides of the cube. On the floor at the entrance to his workstation were baskets laden with coconuts and pineapples. Statues of hula girls and plastic lobsters were strewn across the desk surfaces inside the cubicle.

"I'm an early starter. I'm always the first or second one in the office," remembers Kelly. "So when I walked in on the Monday morning after my vacation, almost nobody was around to see my reaction, which was fine, because I was totally speechless! My jaw was hanging open. I could hardly believe what I was seeing. It made me feel great because everyone had so obviously gone out of their way for me. It was clear my teammates had spent quite some time and effort putting this together, and I knew they wouldn't do that for just anybody. They told me afterwards they figured I would come back to work and be smacked in the face by reality, so they wanted to ease my transition. It sure worked!"

"Kelly really needed the vacation and he was very stressed when he left. We figured he wouldn't be looking forward to coming back to work afterwards," his coworker Dave Josephsen told me. "We wanted to take the edge off his return, and so we thought— let's just extend his vacation at work.

"Kelly always goes out of his way for everyone else, and we all wanted to give him something back in return. He's very caring and feels everyone else's pain, and it was nice to be able to give something back to him. The best thing was, after I told my boss what we were planning, he even let me expense all the bamboo!"

The sensation of joy is one of the most pleasurable feelings imaginable. Joy is a feeling of lightness and playfulness that emanates directly from the heart. When we intentionally reach out to bring joy to the other people in our lives, we find that sense of joy reaches right back to embrace us as well. It feels good to help other people feel good.

We have all heard that "it is more blessed to give than to receive." Many people mistakenly believe that the blessing one gets from giving will be some future blessing. However, anytime we water the seeds of joy and happiness in other people, we are, at the same time, watering our own seeds of joy. The blessing of acting and giving with an open heart is immediate.

On the other hand, when we act selfishly and close our hearts to others, we know at a deep level that we are also being hurtful to ourselves. In times like this, we are saying that what we want and desire for ourselves is more important than what anyone else wants. In so doing, we lose sight of the fact that we are part of the whole of humanity and the needs and interests of other people are intertwined with our own.

The best way to assure that we are traveling merrily down the path of life is to bring others along with us on our journey. When we bring merriment to another person's heart, our own heart becomes merry at the same time.

There can be no greater reward than that.

TWENTY-SIX

Be Outrageous

*Do not fear to be eccentric ... every opinion now
accepted was once eccentric.*

—BERTRAND RUSSELL

W E DON'T USUALLY associate being successful
with being eccentric or outrageous. More likely, we
tend to think that success comes by following convention and doing what is expected. The famous philosopher John
Stuart Mill believed the exact opposite, and I think he may well
have a point.

Mill thought that an organization or society had mental vigor,
creativity, genius, and moral courage in direct proportion to the
amount of eccentricity it possessed.

Our chance of making our lives more successful at work and
creating more happiness and joy in the workplace is in large

measure dependent upon our willingness to be unconventional and unusual.

It is a simple thing to transform your work environment into a play environment if you are open to eccentric and divergent thinking. What if, for example, instead of an office space, you were able to see that you were working in . . . a golf course!

For their entry in a "Fun at Work" contest at Electronic Data Systems, Charleen Hubbell and her team decided to create an eighteen-hole miniature golf course in their offices in Rochester, New York. Each person was responsible for designing his or her own golf hole and for providing prizes for people who got a "hole in one." Outsiders (people not on the design team) were charged a fee to play the course. All the "greens fees" went toward a happy hour where the players met to relax from a tough day at the office links.

Bernie DeKoven, creator of the Deep Fun website, calls this kind of indoor office fairway "subversive golf." Bernie invited subscribers to his weblog to play subversive golf and let him know the results. Following is a report from the website:

"The idea of subversive golf inspired me to disrupt the president's staff meeting this morning to invite them out for a game. The entire (and very startled) twelve-member President's Cabinet followed me out into the hall where I had set up a one-hole subversive golf tournament. Players had to hit from the tea box (a box of Lipton's tea) with their ball on the tea (a tea bag). Most golfers would call the hole a 'dog leg right'; however, we don't like to think of disconnected dog parts, so the hole was a chicken leg to the right into the president's office. (Even though I am a vegetarian, we did have an actual chicken leg on the floor to mark the turn.)

"If the players hit their ball through the chicken leg, then he or she had to hit the next shot out of the trap. (We used the lint trap from my clothes dryer for that.) Obviously, if one went into the trap he or she had to hit out with a wedge rather than a putter. We used a wedge made of cheddar cheese. I got the feeling that several players hit through the chicken leg on purpose, so they could play out of the lint trap with the cheese. Just inside the president's office was the cup (which was one of my treasured Mickey Mouse teacups).

"After the one-hole tournament, we had a 'closest to the pen' contest. Everyone had one putt to see who could come closest to the president's desk pen set.

"In the one-hole tournament the lowest score was 4 and the highest 15; however, I declared that everyone had won, because everyone played. The President's Cabinet returned to their meeting still laughing. Everyone agreed it was deep fun."

Going merrily through our lives at work is not something that necessarily just happens. Creating an environment for laughter and play involves intentional action on our part. Sometimes if we are willing to go against convention and be a little outrageous, then success is as simple as 1, 2, 3, Fore!!

TWENTY-SEVEN

Playing the Fool

It is a profitable thing, if one is wise, to seem foolish.

—AESCHYLUS

I TRAVEL BY PLANE a lot. I always ask for an aisle seat because I like to walk around the plane and stretch my legs without having to climb over the person seated next to me. When I'm flying in coach class, I try to reserve a seat in the exit row. It has more legroom than the other rows—on many planes the exit row in coach class is as spacious as a seat in first class.

Just before takeoff the flight attendant comes by to make sure the passengers in the exit row know their duties in case of an emergency and asks them if they are willing to fulfill those responsibilities. Much of the time the exit rows are filled with passengers who have asked to be seated there.

Veteran flyers have all heard the rap about flying in the exit row so many times that we don't actually need any instruction about our duties. The flight attendants can usually tell when the exit row is filled with experienced fliers, so they don't bother to belabor the safety points beyond fulfilling regulations. On a recent occasion, however, we had a flight attendant who insisted on treating us like we were untrustworthy schoolchildren who were trying to put something over on the teacher. "Do you all understand your duties in the exit row?" she asked us.

We all nodded, bored, that we certainly did.

"And you are able to open the emergency exit in case I am unable to be here to do it?"

We nodded again.

"And you are sure that you can do this?"

Our affirmative nods by now included a little eye rolling to each other.

"You are absolutely sure that you can do this?"

At this point, it was getting tiresome.

"And you've read over the entire safety card and you understand everything that is expected of you? You've read the whole thing?"

I sensed a bit of tension in my fellow passengers. We had already indicated many times over that we were ready, willing, and able to execute our responsibilities. One more question from her about our willingness to pull a door handle, and I could sense that things were going to turn ugly.

At this point the man seated next to me stepped in and saved the day. "I'm so glad you asked us about the safety card," he said in a friendly voice. "There's one part of that card I actually can't understand at all." At this point he reached over and grabbed the safety card out of his seatback. "Let's see," he muttered, reading over the card. "Oh, yes, here it is. Maybe you can help me out with this." He gave a big smile, held the card up for her to see, and pointed to the section written entirely in Japanese. "What, exactly, is this part right here all about?"

I wish I could report that she laughed out loud, but at least she smiled as she walked away, which showed me that she understood his attempt to be playful. His use of humor certainly defused the tension for the rest of us. When this same flight attendant walked by us again fifteen minutes later, she playfully asked him if he needed anything else translated.

What this passenger demonstrated was the age-old technique of "playing the fool." This technique is a simple one: you pretend to understand a lot less about a given situation than is likely, so the person you are talking to is caught off guard. For a brief moment the other person thinks, "He can't possibly be *that* stupid, can he?" Then recognition dawns that you are just playing, and laughter follows for everyone involved.

There is a rich tradition of honoring the fool throughout human history. Many classical writers like Erasmus, Shakespeare, and Aristophanes have portrayed the fool in a positive and empowering way. The fool's role has traditionally been to invite others to take risks, to encourage them to try new things, to leave their zone of safety, and in general to explore life more fully. Most important, the fool helps other people to avoid taking themselves too seriously.

We all have a fool within us wanting to come out to play and to help us go more merrily about our lives. Even in the workplace, where so many people believe they must approach work with a solemn and somber attitude, the fool has a place.

The reason playing the fool can make such a positive contribution to communication at work is that it instantly elicits laughter, which breaks tension. What is this underlying tension usually about in the workplace? Most often it is about "status." There is an ongoing conscious and unconscious jockeying among coworkers in an office for higher status. Status is fluid and it is constantly changing in the moment. If the boss likes my suggestion, my status in the group instantly goes up. If I'm unprepared at a meeting, my status in the group immediately goes down.

The reason people laugh at a fool is simple. When we play the fool with someone, we intentionally take a low-status position relative to them. This creates such turbulence in the system that it usually elicits laughter from the people involved. For just a moment, the fool allows everyone involved to step outside of the ordinary status game. They can then enjoy the bonding that comes from laughing together. That laughter releases the backlog of accumulated tension that comes from constantly having to defend one's place in the organizational hierarchy.

Playing the fool has a long and storied history throughout the ages. That does not mean it is in any way outdated. Now more than ever, the merriment of the fool provides a much-needed benefit in our lives. The fool ultimately brings us closer in our relationships at home, with friends, in the workplace, and even with strangers on an airplane.

So if you are ready to go more merrily through life, then it's time to start being a fool!

TWENTY-EIGHT

The Organization as Fool

If all the fools in this world should die, lordly God,
how lonely I should be.

—MARK TWAIN

SOMETIMES ONLY ONE fool just isn't enough. There are situations where only a team of fools will do.

It is not just individuals who can find great value from playing the fool—groups and organizations can benefit from displaying their fool-like qualities, as well. Organizations that intentionally cultivate boundary-busting activities such as taking risks, trying new things, creating rituals, and laughing together soon discover that they have banished terminal seriousness from their place of business.

Richland College is an excellent example of an organization that has gone to some lengths to celebrate the gifts of the fool. In fact, the annual Richland Convocation of all college employees has been dubbed a modern-day "Feast of Fools."

The "Feast of Fools" was the name given to popular medieval religious festivals, the origins of which were traced to the harvest festivals honoring the Roman god Saturn. In these ceremonies all class distinctions were abolished, and the rules governing sensible behavior were virtually suspended. People in even the highest positions were mocked. It was a day for unreason, marked by license and all sorts of buffoonery. In fact, even in church the traditional "amen" that followed prayers was replaced with an energetic and enthusiastic, "hee-haw!"

Richland College's Feast of Fools was established by campus president Steve Mittelstet some twenty-five years ago and continues under his leadership to this day. Each year the event is anticipated by college employees with great enthusiasm. No one is sure what organized craziness will be the order of the day. One constant is that it will be a time for laughter, play, and celebration while, at the same time, looking at the college's most serious goals and aspirations as an organization.

Like most organizations, Richland College has a set of value statements. The college lists joy among its most important values—"Joy: we value laughter, play, love, kindness, celebration, and joy in our learning and work—taking our learning and work seriously and ourselves lightly." The annual Feast of Fools sets the tone for the entire organization to value joy and happiness throughout the year to come.

On any day of the year, a visitor to the campus might catch a performance by the Richland "Divas," a group made up of about twenty female employees who set their own satirical and lampooning lyrics to popular tunes. The Divas might show up at an important meeting, a retirement party, or the ground-breaking ceremony for a new campus building. One never knows.

A visitor might also get caught up in the "Employee of the Month" parade, a joyful affair that winds its way through the campus with drums beating and music playing, as the marchers locate the honoree for the month. The parade, with all its flourish and fanfare, grows as it picks up participants until it arrives by surprise at the honored employee's workstation—which might be a classroom, the mailroom, or a riding lawn mower. Gifts are presented and citations read, and then everyone returns happily to his or her own workstation.

On any given Friday afternoon, our visitor could witness Helen Noble leading her coworkers from the Continuing Education department in an end-of-the-week "jig of celebration." According to Dean Joyce McKnight-Williams, for nearly a decade Helen has ritually "danced away any bad energy from the week and transformed it into a celebration of accomplishments for the staff." Helen is accompanied by coworkers who feel inspired to join in the dance or to pound out the beat on musical instruments. "We all seem to leave the dance freed from a week that has been filled with hectic and challenging issues, feeling that we are valued and we should celebrate our value," concludes Dean McKnight-Williams.

The Richland College Feast of Fools begins each year with a bold statement—"We have serious business to conduct at this college, but we are going to have lots of fun as we go about those serious goals and objectives." This explains why the Work Like Your Dog Institute, established to create and foster laughter and play in the workplace, found a welcome home on the Richland campus.

In my estimation, it also explains—in some measure—why Richland College has been recognized and honored with so many awards over the years. Recently, for example, Richland has received an award for excellence from the Baldrige National Quality Program. This highly competitive award honors organizational excellence in areas such as leadership, strategic planning, knowledge management, and human resource focus. In the seventeen-year history of this award, presented annually by the president of the United States, Richland is only the third higher education institution to be selected and the only community college ever to have been so honored.

When an organization, big or small, is willing to become the fool, then good things happen. Individuals within the group feel empowered to bring out their own fool, as well. The group that laughs and plays together is headed merrily, merrily, merrily, merrily toward success.

TWENTY-NINE

Toxic Humor

The coward's weapon, poison.

—JOHN FLETCHER

NOT ALL LAUGHTER is created equal.

Too often humor can be used in a way that does not help us to live a life that is merry and successful. This kind of humor is called "toxic humor"—it is like deadly venom that is unhealthy for all involved. Toxic humor is about putting someone else down and making a particular group or individual the butt of the joke.

Toxic humor is based upon a lie. It suggests that some of us are better than others because of our ethnicity, our gender, our religion, our culture, our mental capacities, our sexual orientation, or things as insignificant as our weight or the color of our hair. Instead of bonding us together, toxic humor tears us apart. It is humor that is always based on the idea that one group is superior to another. Sharing humor that insults other people, degrades them, and otherwise debases them is poisonous and never contributes to genuine success.

Unfortunately, this kind of humor appears quite frequently in the workplace. Toxic humor is bad for the well-being of an individual, and you can be sure that it is bad for the health of the organization, as well.

As we have seen, shared laughter at work can be a healthy way to break the ice, release tension, and reduce stress. It is also a fantastic way to bond people together as a team. However, laughter and joking can also be a way to undermine progress, to deflect serious thought, and to express veiled hostility.

Often the words that indicate toxic humor has reared its ugly head are "Can't you take a joke?" Joking behavior can be a shield to hide behind, an indirect way to express anger or fear. When, for example, someone is afraid to confront others openly about something that disturbs him, he instead makes a joke at their expense. This kind of humor gives the joke teller instant deniability. "Hey, what are you getting so upset about? I was just kidding. Can't you take a joke?" asks the cowardly person who is afraid to openly voice his critical judgments and opinions. This is the office coward's way of hiding behind humor as a defense against honest and open communication.

Making a joke about a serious proposal is the easiest way to change the subject. It is a plea to avoid dialogue and disagreement, and most groups have an unspoken norm to avoid confrontation at all costs.

Sometimes it's difficult to tell the difference between a genuine expression of humor and veiled hostility. Sometimes the line between the two is very thin. The key is to ask yourself questions like, "What are the values being expressed in this joking statement? If this person weren't going for the laugh, what would he really be saying? Now that the laughter is over, what is the mood of the group? Are we back on track or are we further afield? What was the intention behind this laughter—to bring us closer together, or to divert our energy in another direction? Even if the intention was good, what actual effect is it having on the situation?"

Coping effectively with the use of toxic humor can be tricky because when you call someone on their inappropriate use of humor they try to deflect the real problem—the use of toxic humor—onto you. They invariably protest that the real problem is simply your lack of a sense of humor.

Not long ago I was having lunch with a man who was trying to convince me that he was the perfect person to manage my retirement portfolio. The nice young woman waiting our table (who happened to be a blonde) got our orders confused, but it was no big deal and was easily corrected.

As soon as she was out of earshot he told me a "dumb blonde" joke. I responded by saying in a gentle but inquisitive tone, "Do you really think that blondes are any less intelligent than anyone else?" He quickly and defensively said, "Oh . . . uh . . . well, it was just a joke!" His underlying message, of course, was "Wow! Don't you have any sense of humor?"

In reality what was going on was not about me or my sense of humor. It was about this man and his inappropriate use of toxic humor. Forget for the moment that I don't share his values. Suppose for example that I wasn't even concerned about his put-down of blondes. Wasn't this joke nevertheless a telling display of poor judgment? For all he knew, my entire family could have been composed of nothing but blonde women! Does he really want to risk the possibility of insulting so many women I care deeply about? Do I really want to entrust my portfolio to someone who exhibits such reckless thinking?

There are thousands of ways we can connect with other people through the use of humor. Toxic humor is not one of them. Living merrily on a path of joy and happiness is a path that leads in the opposite direction from the poisonous trail of toxic humor.

THIRTY

Wrong Time, Wrong Place

I was in the right place, but it must have been
the wrong time.
And I said the right thing, but I must have
used the wrong line.

—MAC REBENNACK, AKA DR. JOHN

I RECENTLY HEARD A gate attendant at the Burbank airport use humor quite effectively to defuse what could have been a tense situation. When I arrived at the gate for my flight, I saw on the monitor that the flight was delayed. A crowd of concerned passengers was gathered around the counter. The gate attendant told us that he would have some news in a few minutes. After a short time he did in fact have news for us—the delay would be only a half hour. He assured us we'd soon be on our way.

As we prepared to board, the gate attendant made an announcement: "I apologize for the delay. I sincerely hope we haven't inconvenienced anyone too much. I'm happy to tell you, however, that I do have some good news—I just learned I saved about three hundred dollars on my car insurance!"

We all had a good laugh and were happily on our way.

Using humor nearly always carries an element of risk. The psychology of humor is quite complex; however, it is safe to say that most humor is based upon some violation or breach of what is expected. The gate attendant's "good news" for the passengers was certainly not expected to be about his own good fortune. So it was funny to us.

Whether or not an attempt at humor is appropriate depends upon the situation. As with so many things in life, timing is essential. Laughter has many benefits, and shared laughter is something that every group needs. There are times, however, when using humor is counterproductive and not at all appropriate. Humor does not have to be toxic to be inappropriate—sometimes it just might be the wrong place and the wrong time.

On a recent business trip to Houston, my flight experienced a combination of weather delays and mechanical problems. The airline kept assuring us that we would be on our way for the brief flight to Houston shortly, but shortly never arrived.

What followed for the passengers was a string of hassles— boarding the plane late, waiting at the gate, and then being told we would have to change to a new plane.

As we all hurried to our new gate, I called my client and told him that the plane was delayed but that everything was now under control. I said I might be as much as an hour late.

"It's all good," he reassured me. "We're not worried. We'll be waiting for you. Just get here as soon as you can."

Finally we boarded the new plane. "Just in time," I thought. "I can still make it. Now, let's go!"

Instead, once again the plane sat at the gate. We waited. Then we waited some more. A half hour passed. The murmured complaints of upset passengers could be heard all around.

Finally the doors closed. The flight attendant's cheerful voice came over the loudspeaker:

> " 'Twas the week before Christmas, and all through the
>   plane
> The passengers to Houston looked out at the rain.
> Fasten your seatbelt and stow your tray table
> And we'll take off just as soon as we're able."

My seatmate and I stared at each other in disbelief. "She's lost her mind!" I said.

"I'm going to strangle someone," he muttered.

"You can start with her!" I replied.

Humor is not a panacea. It is not the answer to everything. There is a time and a place for humorous behavior and this was the perfect example of inappropriate timing. If there was any humor to be found in the situation, it had to come from the passengers, not from the airline. This wasn't a brief delay or a minor inconvenience. This was a major problem for many people, and it required a serious response.

There is a good reason why *Row, Row, Row Your Boat* comes before *Merrily, Merrily, Merrily, Merrily*. As we have seen, taking personal responsibility is a key to achieving success. In the Burbank episode, the gate attendant had in fact taken personal responsibility for the situation before attempting to use humor to defuse the passengers' strained feelings. By first owning up to the airline's part in causing our discomfort, he was able to make the situation appropriate for an effective use of humor.

The attendant on the flight to Houston was trying to use humor to substitute for personal responsibility. What we needed from her first, as a representative of the airline, was an apology—and then another apology, and perhaps another one after that!

Making light of our situation didn't make us feel better—in

fact it made us feel much worse. It made us feel like we weren't being taken seriously as customers and that the airline was not taking any responsibility for all the delays we had suffered. Successful people do not try to use humor to dodge accountability.

Perhaps the flight attendant had received an appreciative reaction in the past for her little rhyme. In another situation it may have been just fine—but not this time.

PART IV

LIFE IS BUT A DREAM

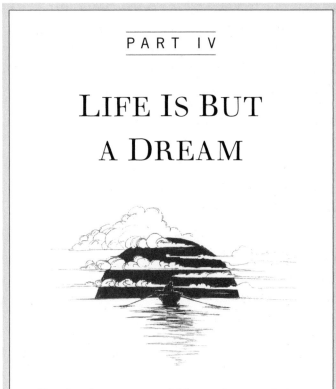

People who are successful know that our choices

always move us closer to or farther away

from what we really want in life. If you want

to be successful in life, then you must

choose the life that will take you there.

You can choose to make your life a nightmare

or a dream.

THIRTY-ONE

Life as a Yardman

If you love what you are doing, you will be successful.

—ALBERT SCHWEITZER

BACK IN MY college days, I was first introduced to the difference between connotation and denotation. My professor said, "You could be buried at Restland Memorial Cemetery, Skyline Memorial Park, or Joe's Graveyard. They all three denote the same thing, but the feeling sure is different!"

The reason the example stuck in my mind was that my uncle Joe's business was called Joe's Lawn and Tree Service. He had hand-painted the sign on the side of his old truck. As soon as I heard my professor's example, I knew that I had to talk to Uncle Joe about what I saw as his "problem with connotation."

I rushed to tell my uncle that I thought he needed a more

sophisticated and important-sounding name for his business. As I recall, I suggested something like "Metropolitan Landscape Architecture."

Uncle Joe just looked at me and shook his head slightly. "Well," he said, "you can call your butt a bass fiddle, but that doesn't mean it will make music!" My uncle was not a man of pretense. Whenever anyone asked him what he did for a living he flatly and proudly said, "I'm a yardman."

Uncle Joe returned to the States after World War II and enrolled at the University of San Francisco. To help with his college expenses he started mowing lawns for the Park Department. I guess that's how he first fell in love with yard work. He graduated with a degree in history, and shortly after that he started his own lawn-mowing service. The rest, as they say, is history.

My uncle Joe gave me my first job, as a lawn-mowing assistant. I never loved the work the way he did. It just seemed like difficult, dirty work to me. I was ready to move on to other vocational callings as soon as the opportunity permitted. Uncle Joe, however, never wanted to do anything else. He had already found his dream job.

My uncle told me that he loved the freedom of his job. He loved being his own boss. He loved working in the outdoors. He loved getting his hands into the soil. He loved making things look nice. He loved, he said, how often he was able to feel that he had finished something. He also loved the fact that when he left his work, he didn't take it home with him.

I think about Uncle Joe a lot when I see so many people who are trying to live a dream life, but it is not their own dream. They have never been in touch with their own dream because they are too caught up in the trance of expectations—especially the expectations of others. They do not love what they are doing. They may not even like what they are doing.

One of the most popular questions asked in this culture is "What do you do?" It is clear that an answer like, "I am a yard-man," will be understood as anything but success. On the other hand, I suspect that you know as many people as I do whose high-status, high-paying, and socially acceptable jobs don't keep their lives from being more nightmare than dream.

Unless your dream is more like my uncle Joe's—one that was chosen because it was what he loved and wanted with internal rather than external motivation—then it has a very good chance of ending up as a nightmare. In order to live life as a dream, what we do is not as important as that we are doing what we really love to do.

Several years ago, I had my own accidental experience as a yardman that reinforced this lesson. My adventure started when I was working in my own yard. I was hot and thirsty, so I went in for a quick drink of water.

While I was in the house I received a phone call that was obviously a wrong number. The woman on the other end of the line said, "Is this the man who does yards?" I found the mistake amusing because at that very moment I was doing my yard, so I said playfully, "Yes, it is. How can I help you?"

The caller explained that she had lost touch with her regular yardman and needed someone to do her yard. She explained further that she had gotten my number from a friend of hers for whom I had worked in the past. So she was wondering if I could do her yard.

I had been playing along this far, so I decided to play it through. I asked, "So how much did I charge to do your friend's yard?" She reported that I had charged thirty-five dollars and that her yard was about the same size.

I then asked her where she lived, and it turned out that she lived less than a mile from my own house. So, figuring that I already had my lawn equipment out and she lived close by, I said, "Sure, I can do your yard."

She replied somewhat hesitantly, "I don't mean to be pushy, but when do you think you can fit me into your schedule?"

I said, "How about right now?"

She was thrilled and said, "Wow! That's great service."

So I loaded up my equipment and drove to her house. She and her husband were really nice people, and I was having fun with my little joke. When I finished, however, she said that she wanted to hire me as her yardman for the rest of the summer. It was at this point that I began to wonder, "Just how much fun do I want to have with this joke?"

I asked her how often she needed her yard mowed, and she said maybe every ten days or two weeks throughout the summer. I figured that I would be doing my own yard that often and that I could just drive up and do her yard each time I did my own. So I said, "Sure, I can be your yardman."

As it turned out, it was a bit more complicated than I had imagined. The next time I arrived to do the yard, she had little extra jobs she wanted me to do—weeding gardens, trimming hedges, and so on. Having no experience with such things, I just sort of pulled prices out of the air. She seemed to like my prices, and so the charade continued throughout the summer.

Near the end of the summer I was invited to a cocktail party at my next-door neighbor's house. He is a bank president and was hosting the party to introduce a candidate for city council. When I walked into the party, whom should I see standing across the room but my one and only customer!

Eventually I walked over to her and we exchanged pleasantries. Never once, however, did she bring up yard work or show any surprise about me being at the party. The next day, however, my neighbor told me about the "strangest" conversation from the previous night. He reported a conversation something like this:

"Can you tell me what *he's* doing here?"

"What do you mean?"

"I'm just surprised to see my yardman at this kind of party!"

"Your yardman?"

"Yes. That man is a yardman. He does my yard."

"I think you must be confused. He's not your yardman. He's a college professor."

"That man right there is my yardman! He's not a professor! He's my yardman!"

"I can assure you he is a college professor. He's my next-door neighbor."

"That's *his* house next door? I can't believe a yardman can afford such a nice house!"

After this, I was a little apprehensive about whether to continue to fulfill my summer obligation; however, I reluctantly returned to do her yard the next time it was due. She was out the door before I could start my mower.

"Excuse me," she said, "but I'm very confused. Bob told me that you are a college professor?"

"Yes," I replied innocently.

"Well, I'm just surprised that you would need to have a second job as a yardman!"

I decided that I needed to straighten things out. On the other hand, I wasn't exactly sure how to explain the whole experience myself. Finally, I told her that I was not actually a yardman but that when she called she had not really asked me if I was a yardman. She had asked if I was the man who did yards. In fact, I did do yards—just mine before she called and now both mine and hers.

She started laughing, and I laughed along with her. We both decided that it was very odd and very funny. Then, I did her yard, she paid me thirty-five dollars, and I went home.

It is an experience that I will never forget. It is an experience that reminds me also of my uncle Joe. Like Uncle Joe, in my brief career as a yardman, I loved what I was doing. Of course, my little private joke was what made it so wonderful for me. On the other hand, there is a great lesson in all this that goes right back to the wisdom of Uncle Joe.

Simply put, our life becomes a dream when we are following a path that we really love—a path we have freely chosen and not one that has been chosen for us. Success is about shaping an external reality that is in harmony with our internal passion. When we have clarity about what real success will be for our own unique self, then, rowing and flowing merrily, we will be able to say with Lewis Carroll, "What is life but a dream?"

THIRTY-TWO

The Importance
of Habit

We are what we repeatedly do. Excellence,
then, is not an act, but a habit.

—ARISTOTLE

A WELL-KNOWN POEM by Portia Nelson depicts a person who walks down the same street and continually falls into the same deep hole in the sidewalk. This poem resonates for many people because we often fall—over and over again—into the same deep holes in our lives. We may not have seen the hole the first time we fell in, but that doesn't seem to stop us from falling into that same old hole all over again. Eventually, we simply fall into the hole out of habit.

In our lives—at home, in relationships, at work, and everywhere else—so much of what we do is primarily "because that's the way we have always done it." Doing things by habit is not in and of itself a bad thing. After all, we are not defined as people by what we do sometimes, occasionally, or when the whim strikes us. We are characterized by what we do habitually. As the ancient philosopher Aristotle had it, "We become just by doing just acts, temperate by doing temperate acts, brave by doing brave acts."

Are there good habits and bad habits? Of course there are, but much of that depends on one's point of view. When I first became a long-distance runner, I was warned about the dangers of dehydration. So during every run I made sure to drink lots and lots of water. Then friends told me that not only runners but everybody should be drinking more water—at least eight big glasses a day in order to be healthy. So I developed the habit of carrying water everywhere with me and drinking whenever I could.

My new mantra became, "Hydrate, hydrate, hydrate." While driving my car, whenever I stopped at a red light, my hand automatically reached for the water bottle. If I was talking with a friend, I reached for my water while listening. If he or she asked me a question, I took a sip while I paused to think of my reply. Whenever I stopped to think, I stopped to drink. Drinking massive quantities of water became second nature to me and I was glad that this was a habit that was changing my life for the better—or was it?

Several years later, I was shocked to discover new research that found that the greatest danger to long-distance runners was not from drinking too little water but from drinking too much water! In this condition, called hyponatremia, water dilutes the blood, which floods into the cells, including the cells of the brain. These swollen brain cells can become fatal. The *New York Times* quoted Dr. Lewis G. Maharam, the medical director for the New York City Marathon, as saying, "There are no reported cases of dehydration causing death in the history of world running, but there are plenty of cases of people dying of hyponatremia."

Now I was running scared! This was one "good" habit I

needed to break right away. As always, it was helpful to find a way to laugh at my dilemma. I was delighted to read the words of W. C. Fields, who was quoted as saying, "I never drink water. I'm afraid it will become habit-forming." My new water guru also pointed out, "I never drink water; that is the stuff that rusts pipes." I was cured of my habit by the time I saw his final quote, "I never drink water because fish poop in it!"

In order to choose a life that is more dream than nightmare, we must realize the enormous influence that habit plays in our lives. As I learned the hard way, we must be ready also to change our old habits when we get new information.

We have heard many times that "practice makes perfect." I think it only takes a moment's reflection to realize that this is decidedly untrue. Just because we do something repeatedly it doesn't follow that it will lead to perfection. If we make the same mistake a thousand times, it doesn't make our life any better! It is much more realistic to think that practice merely leads in the direction of stability and firmness—whether for the better or for the worse.

In the not too distant past, many neuroscientists believed that connections among neurons in the brain were established in the early months of life and that cortical maps were fixed and unalterable. However, contemporary brain research shows that the brain is actually very agile.

This agility in our brain is not brought about by ordinary human development or by inherited traits. The changes, instead, are brought about by changes in the way we behave habitually. Our changes in behavior change the maps in our brain and allow them to support new knowledge and skills. This is why the habits we form are so crucial to our success.

In the same way we become just by doing just acts, so too we become personally responsible by taking responsibility for our own successes and shortcomings. We can become actively engaged in designing the life we want, both at home and at work, by repeatedly envisioning our success and consistently setting goals to make it happen. If we faithfully practice taking risks, expanding our boundaries, and viewing things from multiple and unique perspectives, then that is the kind of person we become. We will "grow" as a person and achieve the success that we are after.

On the other hand, if we are always looking for someone else to blame, continually making excuses, and habitually feeling helpless in the face of it all, then we will keep finding ourselves in the same deep holes, day after day.

Having the dream of a peaceful, unruffled, and serene life involves the daily practice of being peaceful, unruffled, and serene. Intentional, daily practice of going gently down the stream is how our lives become more peaceful and happy. Likewise, the nightmare of stress, anxiety, fretfulness, and all the negative emotions that make us miserable are just as much a matter of habit and practice.

When our days are filled with laughter and play, then our life becomes a dream. When we can lighten up and laugh at ourselves, we can turn nightmares into dreams. We have the choice of habitually suffering the pangs of terminal seriousness—or we can laugh out loud and have the merry heart of the wise fool.

One of the things I have tried to do in this book is to stay focused on Wittgenstein's notion that the most important things are too often hidden from us by their "simplicity." The writer Annie Dillard said it about as simply as it can be put: "How we spend our days is, of course, how we spend our lives."

Living the dream life of success is really in the final analysis about the choices we make every day. We can walk down the same streets and fall into the same deep and nightmarish holes. Or we can form new habits. We are in charge of our own autobiography. We always have the choice to go down a new and different street.

THIRTY-THREE

Keep It Simple

Any intelligent fool can make things bigger, more complex, and more violent. It takes a touch of genius—and a lot of courage—to move in the opposite direction.

—E. F. SCHUMACHER

OCKHAM'S RAZOR IS a classic principle attributed to the fourteenth-century Franciscan friar and philosopher William of Ockham. This idea, which underlies all scientific models and theory building, says that one should not multiply or increase, beyond what is necessary, the number of entities required to explain something. Stated even more simply, if we have two guesses at predicting an answer, choose the simpler explanation.

The idea is that we should "shave off" those hypotheses, solutions, or possibilities that are not really needed to explain any particular phenomenon or event. For example, if we want to travel the most direct route from point A to point B, there are an infinite variety of very complicated ways to go. Ockham's razor would guide us to take the straightest possible route as the best solution.

I recently had a student who suspected his girlfriend, who lived with him, of somehow reading his email. As he reported it to me, he was having a completely platonic relationship with another woman, and they had exchanged a number of messages. His girlfriend became extremely jealous of this relationship. It seemed that she was very aware of the content of his email messages with his platonic female friend.

He finally confronted his girlfriend about the fact that it appeared that she had somehow been reading his email. Eventually she confessed that she had seen some of the messages but explained to him what had happened. She told him that in some inexplicable way his email had been sent to her cell phone in text messages by mistake. She wasn't sure how it had actually happened, but perhaps it was because they lived in the same house, had the same street address, "or something like that."

As we discussed the possibilities, I pulled out Ockham's razor to see if something or someone needed a shave. I said, "What seems more likely to you—that there was a miraculous email cross-up, or that she figured out how to get into your email?"

"How could she have read my email?" he protested. "She doesn't know my password!"

You should know that this student was a diehard Dallas Cowboys fan. He wore Cowboys shirts and hats to class. He loved talking about the Cowboys at every opportunity. At the beginning of each class, I open with the same remark, "Questions? Comments? Complaints? . . . Compliments?" Without fail, this student would blurt out, "Go, Cowboys!" It was funny the first few times; however, after the first week or so, the class appreciated it more for the ritual than for the humor.

"Couldn't she just have figured out your password?" I offered by way of explanation.

"No way!" he protested. "How do you think she could do that?"

"Well," I said, taking a shot in the dark, "could it be anything like 'Go, Cowboys'?"

He looked a bit stunned. "Well, yes," he stammered, "that *is* my password!" Somehow, I think he also had a sudden insight about Ockham's razor regarding his girlfriend's explanation.

I think that there should be an offspring of Ockham's razor that we might call the "Life Is but a Dream" razor. The cutting-edge idea of this razor is that if we really want to have a dream life, then we must seek—at home, in our family, at work, or anywhere else—the simplest way. We must strive to avoid multiplying our burdens beyond what is necessary.

One bit of good news is that much of the complexity that we find in our lives is self-inflicted. Every day we have the choice to make our lives more complex or to make the choice for simplicity. This does not mean, of course, that we can control all of the external factors in our lives—far from it. On the other hand, we are always in charge of how we respond to the things that are presented to us. With every interaction, we can add to the complexity of our lives or we can move in the direction of the uncomplicated.

I think the clearest imperative about living a life that is a dream was provided by the mythologist Joseph Campbell, who said, "Follow your bliss." Campbell believed that when we genuinely follow our bliss, doors to success will open for us that will not open for anyone else. I would not want to complicate a directive as straightforward as "Follow your bliss," unless it is to add, "and keep it simple."

THIRTY-FOUR

Success as Happiness

*Happiness is as a butterfly which, when pursued, is
always beyond our grasp, but which if you will sit
down quietly, may alight upon you.*

—NATHANIEL HAWTHORNE

L IKE A BUTTERFLY flitting from flower to flower, I
was busy networking at a reception at a large business
convention. At one point, a client of mine introduced me
to the director of a major conference for the technology industry.
My client suggested that I would be an excellent speaker for the
upcoming conference, and he added that executives at a high-tech
meeting could probably use an extra-large dose of my teachings
about laughter and play at work.

The conference executive shook her head dubiously. "I just
don't think you would be an appropriate speaker for my people.
This is a very high-level conference, where most of the attendees
have CEO embossed on their business cards."

"Oh, that's no problem!" I replied. "I'm never outranked at any CEO gatherings." With a smile I offered her my Playfair business card on which my own title reads, EMPEROR.

She looked at the card, looked back up at me, looked at the card once again, and then put it away in her purse without any further comment. No laughter, no smile, not a word.

I quickly realized that the conversation was over, and this was one job I was not going to get. Although my title of Emperor did not bring me any work on that particular occasion, it has been of great service to me over the years. More often than not, I get fun responses like, "Well, I'm just going to have to call myself the Queen of Marketing from now on!"

The job titles at Playfair include not only mine as Emperor, but there are also Senior Vice-Emperors, Senior Vice-Empresses, and other nontraditional and outrageous designations. These titles bring a certain kind of lightness and play to our business interactions and to our serious calling of bringing more laughter and play into the workplace.

Do we suddenly become more successful because of our grandiose titles? Not in the conventional sense, no. However, by creating these playful titles we regularly remind ourselves of our deeper purpose, our meaning, and what does bring us authentic happiness—our connection to each other and our ongoing work of bringing joy to others.

On any given day, Playfair may not get any new clients. In any given year, our company may be more or less successful, if success is judged only by external measures such as the bottom line. On the other hand, if being successful means bringing more happiness into our lives and the lives of others, then we can always be considered successful, regardless of our everyday achievements. Clarity of and comfort with our inner purpose sustain us in ways that external achievements cannot.

As you have probably noticed in your own life, there is a

profound correlation between happiness and success. Your life cannot truly be called successful if it does not bring you happiness at the same time. In fact, I believe that success and happiness are the same thing with different names. To be successful, therefore, it does not follow that you need to accomplish all sorts of significant things or receive accolades and honors, as we have already seen with my uncle Joe.

I remember a conversation I once had with him in which I asked my uncle how he felt—being the oldest of seven sons—about having so many really successful brothers. At the time, it didn't occur to me that Uncle Joe might have heard that question as an insult about his own lifelong career as a yardman. However, he just smiled and said, "Yep, all those boys have sure achieved a lot." I noticed that he had changed my assumption about their "success" to the more accurate "achievement."

It did not take me long to realize that Uncle Joe was correct about that—it is not necessary to "achieve" a lot, or for that matter to have any of the conventional trappings of success, in order to be happy and successful. In fact, some of the happiest people I have ever met have almost no possessions at all to speak of.

Several times during the past two decades I have traveled to a small village in southern France to live for a few weeks in retreat in a community led by the Zen teacher Thich Nhat Hanh. On each of these visits, I have been struck by the obvious and plentiful happiness of the residents of that community. Without a doubt, these simple monks and nuns are among the happiest people whom I have ever met.

The monks and nuns have meager possessions. They sleep on the floor. There are no fancy wardrobes or plasma televisions. In fact, there are no televisions at all. By the usual standards that are used in our society, they have nothing. There is one thing, however, that is found in great abundance—joy. Even as a visitor to that peaceful haven, it is easy for me to wake up each morning and say, "Yes, life here is a dream."

In reality, the vast majority of us are not going to spend our lives protected from the travails of everyday life in the tranquility and harmony of a monastery. That does not mean, however, that we cannot choose a life that nourishes and sustains us. If our life is to be a dream, we must first liberate ourselves from the nightmare of chasing after happiness in all the wrong places. Here are some things I have learned about genuine happiness:

- Authentic happiness is not caused by external events or by things such as making money, getting a great job, having the brightest kids, or winning the lottery.

- Happy people are optimistic about how things are going in their lives. They find meaning and joy in what they do, whatever that happens to be.

- The more you look for happiness in external events, the unhappier you are likely to become.

- You can't *find* happiness. Happiness finds you when you live your life in a purposeful way that is uniquely your own.

Even though I have been blessed with a satisfying job, a wife I love, great friends, and many treasured possessions, I have discovered that my happiness and success really don't depend on such things. All those things are in some way external and beyond my control.

Just like dreams in our sleep, a life that results in happiness is ultimately based on our internal life, not our external one. There is something wonderful and magical about our sleeping dreams.

Our dreams can give us a sense of power and a sense of connection with all things. Dreams can bring us joy and liberation. In our dreams we are not bound by the conventional restrictions of time and space—we can fly through the air, speak with the dead, and travel to worlds unknown. There are no limits to our lives in the dream world.

That kind of magic and wonder is available to us in our daily lives, as well. When we free ourselves from external images of happiness and all the limitations that those images entail, we can open our lives to our authentic inner happiness. We can then see that success and happiness are one—the same experience going by different names.

Like a butterfly, success and happiness will alight upon us.

THIRTY-FIVE

Putting the Four Unforgettable Keys into Practice

*Dreams pass into the reality of action. From the actions
stems the dream again; and this interdependence
produces the highest form of living.*

—ANAÏS NIN

IN ONE OF my favorite poems Pablo Neruda writes, "I am weary of chickens." Chickens, he explains, look at us with their small, dry eyes as if we are "unimportant." It is true that we are not very important, but, as others have noted, that news is difficult to take from a "damn chicken." I suppose I never felt as touched by the Neruda poem as I have during this past week. First, let me assure you that this story has a happy ending. Most will agree that it is an odd story, and some will find it even odder than others.

My wife and I agreed to spend several months during the writing of this book house-sitting for our dear friends Marje and

Dick Takei. They were engaged in a variety of preretirement activities—volunteering in New Orleans to serve the victims of Hurricane Katrina, spending a couple of months in Dick's home state of Hawaii, and, in general, living their way into the great question of the narrative called Life, "What happens next?"

You should know that house-sitting for Marje and Dick is more than just watering a few plants and sorting the mail. First of all there are the two wonderful Standard poodles and the kitty that need care. The pigeons, of course, need daily attention, as do the fish. The garden is vast, and then there are the chickens.

When you add in our own two dogs, then life is not exactly simple at the Takeis' house, which is part of the excitement and part of the dread. I suppose if we had been on our toes, then we would have been more concerned about our golden retrievers and their relationship with the chickens.

I was sitting at my computer working on this very book when I heard horrible screaming from outside. My wife was returning from a walk with the dogs, and my writing was interrupted with screams of "No! No! No! *No*, Mead, *no!*" By the time I arrived outside, the damage had been done. My wife was scolding Mead, who had chased after one of the hens that had escaped from the pen into the yard.

These chickens are layers, and they provide eggs for the Takei family and many of their friends. On the other hand, they also have names and are as much pets as producers. My golden retrievers are bird dogs, after all, so it is not surprising that Mead was chasing a chicken or that she had caught one. Mead, of course, knew by our screaming and scolding that she had done something seriously wrong (i.e., be a bird dog), but the worst was yet to come.

My wife discovered that Mead had bitten the chicken. The little fowl clearly had a dog bite in her back, but all her vital organs appeared to be intact. After a quick and unprofessional analysis, my wife decided that the chicken needed to see a vet. It was just after five o'clock, so no regular vets were open. After some hurried phone calling, we located an emergency animal hospital that was able to take us. They warned us on the phone that the fee for an examination would be sixty-four dollars, and that whatever treatment was necessary would be on top of that.

At this point, I made a case to my wife for putting some antibiotic cream on the bird and then letting nature take its course. Admittedly, my argument was weak, and I knew it. My wife quickly convinced me that we had, for a variety of reasons, both the personal and the moral responsibility for what happened. So in short order we were off to the vet with the chicken wrapped in my wife's shirt.

As we drove across town toward the hospital, I tried to lay the whole thing off on the chicken. I said, "You can't expect the dogs not to chase the chickens! Why did the chicken get outside the fence?"

My wife smiled and said, "So you're asking 'Why did the chicken cross the fence?' "

I knew there were at least a thousand answers to that one, but I just grinned and said, "Let's just hope we can save it before it gets to the other side. . . ."

In typical American medical system overkill, we had to fill out three pages—front and back—including one page about the incident and the "medical history" of the chicken, before we could see the vet. We were seen first by a "triage specialist," who thought that the bite was severe enough for stitches, which would mean anesthesia. She assured us, "Chickens usually handle sedation fairly well."

We spent a long time in the waiting room; however, the time passed somewhat more quickly than it might have because there were all those forms to fill out. When I got to the question "name of pet," I realized I didn't know this chicken's name, so I just wrote "Henny Penny."

Eventually we were led to a treatment room, where we waited another half hour for the doctor. The doctor arrived and apologized for the delay. He was the kindest of young men and, very honestly, had a wonderful chicken-side manner. He gave little Henny Penny a complete and gentle checkup. At one point he looked up, smiled, and said, "She's working on a pretty good egg here!"

The doctor pronounced her in great health with the exception of the wound in her back. He said that he thought she would be fine but she would need to have the cut stitched, which meant she would have to be put under anesthesia. He also told us that she needed to be on an antibiotic for a short time, but that afterward she should be as good as new.

His postexamination report included an amazing understanding of chicken depth psychology. He explained that chickens know in their "subconscious" that they are prey. So, when they are injured, they try to fake like they are not, so that no one will know they are more vulnerable than usual. For that reason, he said, "You will have to make sure that she is safe and warm for several days after the surgery." He really appeared to like Henny Penny. He called her by name several times and commented about how calm she was when being held, compared to other chickens he had handled.

He told us that he had another brief examination to do on another patient and that a member of the staff would come in to discuss Henny Penny's "health treatment plan." After the doctor left, I remarked to my wife that perhaps he thought the chicken had insurance!

My wife replied calmly, "They just want to make sure that we are aware of the costs and that there are no surprises."

Meanwhile, I did some quick calculations: at an average of

three to four eggs per week (even at three dollars per dozen for free-range eggs), it was going to take more than three years to recover in egg value the hundred dollars or so that I figured we would have to pay for Henny Penny's stitch job.

Upon announcing the calculations to my wife and, once again, offering that maybe we ought to have opted for the antibiotic cream, she said firmly but kindly, "That's not really the point! It's our responsibility to take care of this chicken!" I felt a little ashamed at being so insensitive and sat back silently to wait for the impending discussion of the "health treatment plan."

After another fifteen minutes of waiting, a young woman came in and placed a computer-generated sheet on the examination table. She then began to go over the charges for "Henny Penny's surgery." My eyes drifted to the bottom line. I heard a voice saying, ". . . this includes the sixty-four-dollar charge for the initial exam"; however, the bottom line was screaming out at me, "Four hundred and ninety-two dollars!" I glanced at my wife, and by the look on her face I could tell that she, too, had seen the bottom line and heard the scream.

"I think we will have to consider some other options," she said gently. "What other options do we have?" I was glad that my wife was the first to speak, as I was almost speechless. The young woman said that she understood and would check with the doctor. As soon as she left I said, "I'm sorry, Henny Penny, but I think we are going to have to consider palliative care, if you get my drift." I again made the case to my wife that we should head home and go for the antibiotic cream. I said, "I know Marje and Dick would do the same thing. They would never spend five hundred bucks to stitch up a chicken! We can buy them ten replacement chickens for that much."

"We can't take a chance that she would suffer," my wife said, and added that it might be best to have the chicken euthanized.

"I can do it," I said flatly. I remembered as a young boy watching my father twirl chickens and snap their heads off. I could never forget that boyhood image of seeing them run around without their heads. My wife grimaced when I told her the story. "Maybe I could do it with an ax," I offered. "I just don't think I could wring her neck."

"I don't want you to have to experience that," she replied. "We'll just have them put her to sleep."

By now we had been in the consultation room for well over an hour. The young woman returned and said that the doctor thought that he could "cut costs a little" and that he could do the surgery for about $350. My wife said that she appreciated his help, but we needed to know about euthanizing the chicken. We had decided that was the best option available to us.

Another half hour passed and the doctor returned. He said that he understood that "different people have different budgets." I wanted to protest and explain that the issue was much more complex than a budget; however, I just nodded. It was at this point that our chicken nightmare was suddenly transformed into a dream. The doctor said, "Actually, there is one more option that we could consider if you are interested."

For some reason, I was absolutely certain that he was going to say that we could just give her some antibiotics and see if she survived. At least that would be an improvement over an antibiotic cream. However, I was pretty sure that my wife would nix that idea. I could almost hear her say, "We can't take a chance on this chicken suffering."

We were a little stunned when the doctor said, "My wife and I are about to start raising some chickens. We have all the books and everything. I would be willing to do the surgery at no cost if you are willing to surrender the chicken."

In response, I actually laughed out loud. I'm not sure now if my laughter was a release of tension, happiness about this wonderful turn of events, or merely brought on by the phrase "surrender the chicken"!

We gleefully agreed to the doctor's proposal. He said that his assistant would return with the paperwork shortly. I said to my wife, "That may have been the easiest choice I have ever made in my life!" We could either pay them sixty-four dollars plus the cost of euthanizing Henny Penny, or else she gets the surgery for free and gets to live. "Oh, no," I joked to my wife, "let's just kill the chicken and pay them a hundred dollars!"

With great delight I signed the paper surrendering the chicken. We were even more delighted when the assistant said, "You don't have to pay the sixty-four-dollar fee. All the medical costs are taken care of."

As I reflected on the experience the next day, I realized that the way in which my wife had handled the entire situation was a perfect example of how to put the simple principles expressed in this book into action.

From the outset, she was rowing her own boat, even though she found herself in a boat that was not of her choosing. Once in the boat, however, she immediately started to row in the direction of a solution to our problem. She took personal responsibility for what happened and took action. While I was busy trying to blame the chicken, she was busy rowing toward a solution.

She was able to flow gently down the stream. She remained open and flexible. Her first conclusion was that we must do all that we could to save the chicken. However, when that option was not feasible, she was able to go with the flow, remain calm, and flow in a new and different direction, even if it meant the chicken had to die.

Throughout the experience she went merrily, merrily, merrily, merrily about doing what needed to be done. She was able to stay lighthearted and playful, without ever betraying her serious commitment to save the chicken. She was able to laugh about the situation and also to laugh at herself.

As has been my attempt to show throughout this book, this is exactly how we can achieve success in our lives. This is precisely how we can choose a life that is truly an everyday dream of happiness. Living in this way will not make things perfect; however, when things do go wrong, this is a path that will help us to transform our nightmares into the dream-life of success.

We laughed a lot about our adventure on our ride home in the car. We had been hours at the clinic, so we decided to stop for dinner. When the waitress took my order for a large Caesar salad she asked, "Would you like that salad with or without the chicken breast?"

My wife and I both broke into huge grins. I looked at the waitress and said, "Without, please." Then I added, "I am weary of chickens."